THE LIGHT at the end of the TUNNEL is an oncoming TRAIN

AND **947** OTHER PITHY PRONOUNCEMENTS
ON LIFE FROM THE CYNICAL SIDE
OF THE TRACKS

STEPHEN WICKS

**Andrews McMeel
Publishing**

Kansas City

01 02 03 04 05 MVP 10 9 8 7 6 5 4 3 2 1

LIBRARY OF CONGRESS CATALOGING-IN-PUBLICATION DATA
THE LIGHT AT THE END OF THE TUNNEL IS AN ONCOMING TRAIN : AND 947 OTHER PITHY
PRONOUNCEMENTS ON LIFE FROM THE CYNICAL SIDE OF THE TRACKS / [COLLECTED BY]
STEPHEN WICKS.
     P. CM.
INCLUDES BIBLIOGRAPHICAL REFERENCES.
ISBN 0-7407-1881-9
     1. QUOTATIONS, ENGLISH. 2. WIT AND HUMOR. I. WICKS, STEPHEN.

PN6084.H8 L54 2001
082—DC21

2001022769

——————— ATTENTION: SCHOOLS AND BUSINESSES ———————
ANDREWS MCMEEL BOOKS ARE AVAILABLE AT QUANTITY DISCOUNTS WITH BULK PURCHASE
FOR EDUCATIONAL, BUSINESS, OR SALES PROMOTIONAL USE. FOR INFORMATION, PLEASE
WRITE TO: SPECIAL SALES DEPARTMENT, ANDREWS MCMEEL PUBLISHING,
4520 MAIN STREET, KANSAS CITY, MISSOURI 64111.

I'm not sure why we're here,
but I'm pretty sure it's not to enjoy ourselves.

LUDWIG WITTGENSTEIN

CONTENTS

CONTENTS

CONTENTS

Introduction

During her final years, Dorothy Parker became increasingly addicted to alcohol. Admitted to a hospital, Parker told the doctor that she would need to leave every hour or so for a drink. The doctor was less than amused by her glib remark and warned Parker that she would be dead in a month if she didn't stop drinking. The noted writer was unimpressed. "Promises, promises," she sighed.

It is often said that comedy and tragedy are two sides of the same coin, and that the best humor is born of life's inevitable misfortunes. Without a doubt, most of the cleverest and most memorable comic lines of all time are sharp rebuttals to life's blackest moments. Dorothy Parker belonged to that unique breed whose keen insight and razor-sharp wit flip the coin and amuse us in the face of our existential angst. No matter what you call these gifted commentators on the human condition—curmudgeons, cynics, grouches, or misanthropes—it is impossible to resist their witty, timeless, and often brilliant observations on every subject from the frustratingly mundane to the profoundly dark.

Here are nearly a thousand of the best quips, quotations, criticisms, and observations from hundreds of the wisest and wittiest minds of the past and present. Sometimes blunt—but always resonating with a dose of reality—these sharp and cantankerous quotations take aim at everything from relationships and politics to cats and vegetarians.

If you've ever paused to reflect on the absurdity of existence and just how unfair life can be, or if you've ever found yourself exasperated by the irritations of life at the turn of the century—cell phones, pet psychiatrists, airline food, lawyers, or whatever irks you most—you'll find plenty of company on the following pages.

Life deals all of us a bad hand now and then, and the human race never fails to remind us of its shortcomings. If life is a disease, as many cynics have proposed, then the quotations collected in this volume offer plenty of evidence that laughter is the best medicine.

CHAPTER 1

OPTIMISM AND PESSIMISM, CYNICISM AND IDEALISM

If you're not cynical, you're stupid.

PAUL ZIMMERMAN, AMERICAN SCREENWRITER

"Know thyself"? If I knew myself, I'd run away.

JOHANN WOLFGANG VON GOETHE

Sixty minutes of thinking of any kind is bound
to lead to confusion and unhappiness.

JAMES THURBER

Cynicism is an unpleasant way of saying the truth.

LILLIAN HELLMAN

Instant gratification takes too long.

CARRIE FISHER

No one ever really minds seeing a friend
fall off a roof.

CONFUCIUS

Preparing for the worst is an activity
I have taken up since I turned thirty-five,
and the worst actually began to happen.

DELIA EPHRON

It was such a lovely day
I thought it a pity to get up.

W. SOMERSET MAUGHAM

Optimist: a proponent of the doctrine
that black is white.

AMBROSE BIERCE

Thank you, but I have other plans.

PAUL FUSSELL, SUGGESTED RESPONSE TO
"HAVE A NICE DAY"

When suffering knocks at your door and
you say there is no seat for him, he tells you
not to worry because he has brought his own stool.

CHINUA ACHEBE, NIGERIAN NOVELIST

Optimist: a man who calls bullshit fertilizer.

FRANK DANE

The cynics are right nine times out of ten.

H. L. MENCKEN

I am kind of a paranoiac in reverse;
I suspect people of plotting to make me happy.

J. D. SALINGER

After a year in therapy, my psychiatrist said to me,
"Maybe life isn't for everyone."

LARRY BROWN, AMERICAN NOVELIST

Am I just cynical, or does anyone else think
the only reason Warren Beatty decided to have
a child is so he can meet babysitters?

DAVID LETTERMAN

The multitude is always in the wrong.

WENTWORTH DILLON, EARL OF ROSCOMMON, 1684

Ninety percent of everything is crap.

THEODORE STURGEON

I find nothing more depressing than optimism.

PAUL FUSSELL

I am free of all prejudice. I hate everyone equally.

W. C. FIELDS

Idealism increases in direct proportion
to one's distance from the problem.

JOHN GALSWORTHY

A grouch escapes so many little annoyances
that it almost pays to be one.

KIN HUBBARD

My one regret in life is that I am not someone else.

WOODY ALLEN

An optimist is a fellow who thinks
a housefly is looking for a way out.

GEORGE JEAN NATHAN

No matter how cynical you get,
it's impossible to keep up.

LILY TOMLIN

The idealist is incorrigible; if he is thrown out of
his heaven he makes an ideal of his hell.

FRIEDRICH WILHELM NIETZSCHE

You've no idea what a poor opinion I have
of myself—and how little I deserve it.

W. S. GILBERT

The power of accurate observation is commonly
called cynicism by those who have not got it.

GEORGE BERNARD SHAW

You can get more with a kind word and a gun than you can with a kind word alone.

AL CAPONE

Objection, evasion, distrust, and irony are signs of health. Everything absolute belongs to pathology.

FRIEDRICH WILHELM NIETZSCHE

A pessimist is one who has been intimately acquainted with an optimist.

ELBERT HUBBARD

There are books in which the footnotes or comments scrawled by some reader's hand in the margin are more interesting than the text. The world is one of these books.

GEORGE SANTAYANA

Those were the good old days—
I was so unhappy then.

CLAUDE CARLOMAN DE RULHIERE

The horror of getting up is unparalleled,
and I am filled with amazement every morning
when I find that I have done it.

LYTTON STRACHEY

Don't look back. Something may be gaining on you.

SATCHEL PAIGE (ATTRIBUTED)

The basis of optimism is sheer terror.

MARK TWAIN

My pessimism goes to the point of suspecting
the sincerity of the pessimists.

JEAN ROSTAND

The wickedness of the world is so great
you have to run your legs off to avoid
having them stolen from under you.

BERTOLT BRECHT

Getting out of bed in the morning
is an act of false confidence.

JULES FEIFFER, AMERICAN PLAYWRIGHT

Opinion has caused more trouble on this little earth
than plagues or earthquakes.

VOLTAIRE

Cheer up, the worst is yet to come.

PHILANDER CHASE

Enough.

AMBROSE BIERCE, DEFINITION OF *ONCE*

Of all the thirty-six alternatives,
running away is best.

CHINESE PROVERB

There are moments when everything goes well.
Don't be frightened—it won't last.

JULES RENARD

Status quo. Latin for the mess we're in.

JEVE MOORMAN

Maturity: A stoic response to endless reality.

CARRIE FISHER

No good deed goes unpunished.

CLARE BOOTHE LUCE

Sanity is a cozy lie.

SUSAN SONTAG

Winter is nature's way of saying, "Up yours."

ROBERT BYRNE, AMERICAN WRITER

Never face facts; if you do you'll
never get up in the morning.

MARLO THOMAS

A Smith & Wesson beats four aces.

AMERICAN PROVERB

Even paranoids have real enemies.

DELMORE SCHWARTZ

Schizophrenia beats dining alone.

ANONYMOUS

Next week or next month, or next year,
I will kill myself. But I might as well last out
my month's rent, which has been paid up.

JEAN RHYS

Is sloppiness in speech caused by ignorance
or apathy? I don't know and I don't care.

WILLIAM SAFIRE

If you're going to do something tonight that
you'll be sorry for tomorrow morning, sleep late.

HENNY YOUNGMAN

CHAPTER 2

LIFE AND DEATH, BIRTH AND IMMORTALITY

Is there life before death?

ANONYMOUS

Immortality: The condition of a dead man
who doesn't believe he's dead.

H. L. MENCKEN

Life is what happens to you
while you're making other plans.

JOHN LENNON

Birth: the first and direst of all disasters.

AMBROSE BIERCE

Look out for yourself—or they'll pee on your grave.

LOUIS B. MAYER

Life may have no meaning. Or even worse,
it may have a meaning of which I disapprove.

ASHLEIGH BRILLIANT, ENGLISH-AMERICAN WRITER

If you die in an elevator,
be sure to press the UP button.

SAM LEVENSON, AMERICAN HUMORIST

I've come to realize that life is not a
musical comedy, it's a Greek tragedy.

BILLY JOEL

Suicide is no more than a trick
played on the calendar.

TOM STOPPARD, AMERICAN PLAYWRIGHT

Pain is life.

CHARLES LAMB

I have an existential map. It has
"You are here" written all over it.

STEVEN WRIGHT, AMERICAN COMEDIAN

For most men life is a search for the proper
manila envelope in which to get themselves filed.

CLIFTON FADIMAN, AMERICAN WRITER

I don't believe in an afterlife, so I don't have
to spend my whole life fearing hell, or fearing
heaven even more. For whatever the tortures
of hell, I think the boredom of heaven
would be even worse.

ISAAC ASIMOV

It is after you have lost your teeth
that you can afford to buy steaks.

PIERRE-AUGUSTE RENOIR

Life is not having been told that the man
has just waxed the floor.

OGDEN NASH

Soon you will have forgotten the world,
and the world will have forgotten you.

MARCUS AURELIUS

The first hundred years are the hardest.

WILSON MIZNER, AMERICAN HUMORIST

Dying is a very dull, dreary affair. And my advice
to you is to have nothing whatever to do with it.

W. SOMERSET MAUGHAM

Being born is like being kidnapped.
And then sold into slavery.

ANDY WARHOL

Life is a goddamned, stinking, treacherous game
and nine hundred and ninety-nine men
out of a thousand are bastards.

THEODORE DREISER

My life has a superb cast
but I can't figure out the plot.

ASHLEIGH BRILLIANT, ENGLISH-AMERICAN WRITER

Don't take life too seriously.
You'll never get out alive.

ANONYMOUS

If people concentrated on the really important
things in life, there'd be a shortage of fishing poles.

DOUG LARSON, AMERICAN WRITER

If I knew I was going to live this long,
I'd have taken better care of myself.

MICKEY MANTLE

I'm trying to arrange my life
so I don't have to be present.

ANONYMOUS

Life goes on forever like the gnawing of a mouse.

EDNA ST. VINCENT MILLAY

We who are about to die, are going to take
one hell of a lot of the bastards with us.

JOEL ROSENBERG, AMERICAN WRITER

One cannot live forever by ignoring
the price of coffins.

ERNEST BRAMAH, ENGLISH WRITER

The secret of life is honesty and fair dealing.
If you can fake that, you've got it made.

GROUCHO MARX

Half our life is spent trying to find something
to do with the time we have rushed through life
trying to save.

WILL ROGERS

There is a remedy for everything; it is called death.

PORTUGUESE PROVERB

He's turned his life around. He used to be
miserable and depressed, now he's depressed
and miserable.

DAVID FROST, ENGLISH TELEVISION HOST

You fall out of your mother's womb, you crawl across open country under fire, and drop into your grave.

QUENTIN CRISP

Perhaps there is no life after death ...
there's just Los Angeles.

RICH ANDERSON

Life is like an onion: you peel off layer after layer and then you find there's nothing in it.

FRENCH PROVERB

Death: to stop sinning suddenly.

ANONYMOUS

Like most endeavors, life is seriously overadvertised and underfunded.

ANONYMOUS

My mother groan'd, my father wept,
Into the dangerous world I lept.

WILLIAM BLAKE

Life is an effort that deserves a better cause.

KARL KRAUS, AUSTRIAN WRITER

Regret to inform you that the hand
that rocked the cradle kicked the bucket.

REPORTED TELEGRAM, IN *NED SHERRIN IN HIS ANECDOTAGE*

So little time and so little to do.

OSCAR LEVANT, AMERICAN ACTOR AND WRITER

We come. We go. And in between
we try to understand.

ROD STEIGER, AMERICAN ACTOR

Life is a dead-end street.

H. L. MENCKEN

I am ready to meet my Maker. Whether my Maker is prepared for the great ordeal of meeting me is another matter.

WINSTON CHURCHILL

He that is not handsome at twenty, nor strong at thirty, nor rich at forty, nor wise at fifty, will never be handsome, strong, rich, or wise.

GEORGE HERBERT

The only good thing about aging is you're not dead.

LILLIAN HELLMAN

Life is something to do when you can't get to sleep.

FRAN LEBOWITZ, AMERICAN WRITER AND HUMORIST

He had decided to live forever or die in the attempt.

JOSEPH HELLER

Live every day as if it were your last, and then someday you'll be right.

ANONYMOUS

When you don't have any money, the problem is food. When you have money, it's sex. When you have both it's health. If everything is simply jake, then you're frightened of death.

J. P. DONLEAVY, AMERICAN NOVELIST

If A is success in life, then A equals x plus y plus z. Work is x; y is play; and z is keeping your mouth shut.

ALBERT EINSTEIN

Life would be tolerable but for its amusements.

GEORGE BERNARD SHAW

There is no such thing as inner peace. There is only
nervousness or death. Any attempt to prove
otherwise constitutes unacceptable behavior.

FRAN LEBOWITZ, AMERICAN WRITER AND HUMORIST

We are all serving life sentences
in the dungeon of life.

CYRIL CONNOLLY, ENGLISH CRITIC

It is now life and not art that requires
the willing suspension of disbelief.

LIONEL TRILLING, AMERICAN CRITIC

I want to die young and at an advanced age.

MAX LERNER

When I die I want to decompose in a barrel of
porter and have it served in all the pubs in Dublin.

J. P. DONLEAVY, AMERICAN NOVELIST

Memorial service: a farewell party
for someone who has already left.

ROBERT BYRNE, AMERICAN WRITER

Moderation in all things. Not too much of life.
It often lasts too long.

H. L. MENCKEN

Life is a shit sandwich and every day
you take another bite.

JOE SCHMIDT, PROFESSIONAL FOOTBALL PLAYER

Good career move.

GORE VIDAL, ON THE DEATH OF TRUMAN CAPOTE

Even death is unreliable; instead of zero
it may be some ghastly hallucination,
such as the square root of minus one.

SAMUEL BECKETT, IRISH NOVELIST AND DRAMATIST

There's no need to worry—
whatever you do, life is hell.

WENDY COPE, ENGLISH POET

Life is generally something that happens elsewhere.

ALAN BENNETT, ENGLISH PLAYWRIGHT

Life is a sexually transmitted disease.

ANONYMOUS

Death will be a great relief. No more interviews.

KATHARINE HEPBURN

Life is divided up into the horrible
and the miserable.

WOODY ALLEN

[Immortality is] to desire the perpetuation
of a great mistake.

ARTHUR SCHOPENHAUER, GERMAN PHILOSOPHER

Life is like playing a violin solo in public and
learning the instrument as one goes on.

SAMUEL BUTLER, ENGLISH WRITER

We're all in this alone.

LILY TOMLIN

Life is a tragedy when seen in close-up
but a comedy in long shot.

CHARLIE CHAPLIN

I often wonder how I'm going to die.
You don't want to embarrass friends.

CARY GRANT

Life is one long process of getting tired.

SAMUEL BUTLER, ENGLISH WRITER

Life is like that old Spanish saying:
"He who plants the lettuce doesn't always
get to eat the salad."

ANTHONY QUINN

Die? I should say not, dear fellow.
No Barrymore would allow such a conventional
thing to happen to him.

JOHN BARRYMORE, AMERICAN ACTOR

Life is like an overlong drama
through which we sit being nagged
by the vague memory of having read the reviews.

JOHN UPDIKE

[Birth is] our first experience of anxiety.

SIGMUND FREUD

Life is not so bad if you have plenty of luck,
a good physique, and not too much imagination.

CHRISTOPHER ISHERWOOD, ENGLISH NOVELIST

Life is wasted on the living.

DOUGLAS ADAMS, AMERICAN WRITER

Not only is life a bitch,
but she's always having puppies.

ANONYMOUS

I detest life-insurance agents; they always argue that I shall some day die, which is not so.

STEPHEN LEACOCK, CANADIAN ECONOMIST AND HUMORIST

Memorial services are the cocktail parties of the geriatric set.

RALPH RICHARDSON, ENGLISH ACTOR

My kid's idea of a hard life is to live in a house with only one phone.

GEORGE FORMAN

Oh, isn't life a terrible thing, thank God!

DYLAN THOMAS

I still go up my forty-four steps two at a time, but that is in hopes of dropping dead at the top.

A. E. HOUSMAN, ENGLISH POET AND SCHOLAR

Life is like a dog-sled team. If you ain't
the lead dog, the scenery never changes.

LEWIS GRIZZARD, AMERICAN COLUMNIST

Sleep is good, death is better, but of course
the real miracle is never to have been born at all.

HEINRICH HEINE, GERMAN POET

Life goes on even for those of us who are
divorced, broke, and sloppy.

NEIL SIMON

When we are born we cry that we are come ...
to this great stage of fools.

WILLIAM SHAKESPEARE

Death is nature's way of saying, "Your table's ready."

ROBIN WILLIAMS

It's not true that life is one damn thing after another—it's one damn thing over and over.

EDNA ST. VINCENT MILLAY

Life is too short to stuff a mushroom.

SHIRLEY CONRAN, ENGLISH DESIGNER AND JOURNALIST

Of all escape mechanisms, death is the most efficient.

H. L. MENCKEN

Why is it that we rejoice at a birth and grieve at a funeral? Because we are not the person involved.

MARK TWAIN

People find life entirely too time-consuming.

STANISLAW J. LEC, POLISH WRITER

My husband and I are either going to buy
a dog or have a child. We can't decide whether
to ruin our carpet or ruin our lives.

RITA RUDNER, AMERICAN COMEDIAN

I don't believe people die. They just go uptown.
To Bloomingdale's. They just take longer
to get back.

ANDY WARHOL

Life is a whim of several billion cells
to be you for a while.

ANONYMOUS

The first half of our life is ruined by our parents
and the second half by our children.

CLARENCE DARROW

Years ago, I came up with what I was going
to say to an assassin if he came to shoot me....
"Thanks for not coming sooner!"

TED TURNER

The first requisite for immortality is death.

STANISLAW J. LEM, POLISH WRITER

I think it's better not to have been born at all.
But how many people do you meet in a lifetime
who were that lucky?

YIDDISH SAYING

I wouldn't mind being dead—
it would be something new.

ESTELLE WINWOOD AT AGE 100, QUOTED IN
INTERNATIONAL HERALD TRIBUNE

For a long time, I focused on the disposal of
my body. It'd be a relief to die in an explosion—
that would take care of the problem.

CANDICE BERGEN

Don't look forward to the day when you
stop suffering, because when it comes
you'll know that you're dead.

TENNESSEE WILLIAMS

My life's dream has been a perpetual nightmare.

VOLTAIRE

Life is like a B-movie. You don't want
to leave in the middle of it
but you don't want to see it again.

TED TURNER

Death is a low chemical trick played
on everybody except sequoia trees.

ANONYMOUS

For three days after death, hair and fingernails
continue to grow but phone calls taper off.

JOHNNY CARSON

May your soul be tormented by fire
and your bones be dug up by dogs and dragged
through the streets of Minneapolis.

GARRISON KEILLOR

In spite of the cost of living, it's still popular.

KATHY NORRIS, AMERICAN WRITER

Life is a roller coaster. Try to eat a light lunch.

DAVID A. SCHMALTZ, AMERICAN WRITER

Always go to other people's funerals,
otherwise they won't come to yours.

YOGI BERRA

I'm amazed he was such a good shot.

NOËL COWARD, UPON BEING TOLD
THAT HIS ACCOUNTANT HAD SHOT HIMSELF

The difference between sex and death
is that with death you can do it alone
and no one is going to make fun of you.

WOODY ALLEN

Millions long for immortality
who do not know what to do with themselves
on a Sunday afternoon.

SUSAN ERTZ, AMERICAN NOVELIST

I do not believe in an afterlife, although I am
bringing a change of underwear.

WOODY ALLEN

It's a good thing that life
is not as serious as it seems to a waiter.

DON HEROLD, AMERICAN WRITER

CHAPTER 3

NINE TO FIVE

EDUCATION, WORK AND BUSINESS,
SUCCESS AND FAILURE, MONEY AND TAXES

My office hours are twelve to one
with an hour off for lunch.

GEORGE S. KAUFMAN, AMERICAN PLAYWRIGHT

Everything worth having is either owned
by bastards or the descendents of bastards.

GREGORY NUNN

I have never liked working.
To me a job is an invasion of privacy.

DANNY MCGOORTY

As Oscar Wilde should have said,
when bad ideas have nowhere else to go, they go
to America and become university courses.

FREDERIC RAPHAEL

If you're not confused, you're not paying attention.

THE WALL STREET JOURNAL

Creativity always dies a quick death in rooms
that house conference tables.

BRUCE HERSHENSOHN

A muttonhead, after an education at West Point—
or Harvard—is a muttonhead still.

THEODORE ROOSEVELT

True you can't take it with you, but then,
that's not the place where it comes in handy.

BRENDAN FRANCIS, ENGLISH WRITER

God made the Idiot for practice, and then
He made the School Board.

MARK TWAIN

A study of economics usually reveals that the best
time to buy anything was last year.

MARTY ALLEN

The purpose of a liberal education is to make you
philosophical enough to accept the fact that
you will never make much money.

NORMAN DOUGLAS

The quickest way to make a million
is to start your own religion.

L. RON HUBBARD

Success and failure are both difficult to endure.
Along with success come drugs, divorce, fornication,
bullying, travel, medication, depression, neurosis,
and suicide. With failure comes failure.

JOSEPH HELLER

For every person wishing to teach
there are thirty not wishing to be taught.

W. C. SELLAR AND R. J. YEATMAN, *AND NOW ALL THIS*

Everyone has a right to a university degree in
America, even if it's in Hamburger Technology.

CLIVE JAMES, AUSTRALIAN AUTHOR

The graveyards are full of indispensable men.

CHARLES DE GAULLE

It is better to have loafed and lost
than never to have loafed at all.

JAMES THURBER

University politics are vicious precisely because
the stakes are so small.

HENRY KISSINGER

Time spent in the advertising business seems to create a permanent deformity like the Chinese habit of foot-binding.

DEAN ACHESON, U.S. ATTORNEY, STATESMAN

If you had your life to live over again— you'd need more money.

CONSTRUCTION DIGEST

A university is what a college becomes when the faculty loses interest in students.

JOHN CIARDI

This is a test. It is only a test. Had it been an actual job, you would have received raises, promotions, and other signs of appreciation.

ANONYMOUS

The average schoolmaster is and always must
be essentially an ass, for how can one imagine
an intelligent man engaging in so
puerile an avocation?

H. L. MENCKEN

Someday I want to be rich. Some people get
so rich they lose all respect for humanity.
That's how rich I want to be.

RITA RUDNER, AMERICAN COMEDIAN

The human race is faced with a cruel choice:
work or daytime television.

ANONYMOUS

We're a trillion dollars in debt. Who do we owe
this money to? Someone named Vinnie?

ROBIN WILLIAMS

One of the great privileges of the great is
to witness catastrophes from a terrace.

JEAN GIRAUDOUX, FRENCH WRITER

Fifteen cents of every twenty-cent stamp
goes for storage.

LOUIS RUKEYSER

College isn't the place to go for ideas.

HELEN KELLER

Few great men could pass personnel.

PAUL GOODMAN, AMERICAN SOCIAL CRITIC

Look at me: I worked my way up from nothing
to a state of extreme poverty.

GROUCHO MARX

A memorandum is written not to inform the reader
but to protect the writer.

DEAN ACHESON, U.S. ATTORNEY AND STATESMAN

If you think nobody cares whether you're dead
or alive, try missing a couple of car payments.

ANN LANDERS

I was fired from my job at Howard Johnson's
when someone asked me the ice cream flavor
of the week and I said, "Chicken."

MIKE NICHOLS

Ambition is a poor excuse for not having
sense enough to be lazy.

CHARLIE MCCARTHY

Gold-tipped cigarettes are awfully expensive;
I can afford them only when I am in debt.

OSCAR WILDE

Our major universities are now stuck with
an army of pedestrian, toadying careerists,
Fifties types who wave around Sixties banners
to conceal their record of ruthless, beaverlike
tunneling to the top.

CAMILLE PAGLIA

Blessed are the young, for they shall inherit
the national debt.

HERBERT HOOVER

Everybody who is incapable of learning
has taken to teaching.

OSCAR WILDE

If it's a bill, the post office will get it to you
in twenty-four hours, if it's a check,
allow them a couple of weeks.

RICHARD NEEDHAM

Business conventions are important because
they demonstrate how many people
a company can operate without.

JOHN KENNETH GALBRAITH

Try not to have a good time ...
this is supposed to be educational.

CHARLES SCHULZ

I am not an economist. I am an honest man!

PAUL MCCRACKEN

The optimum committee has no members.

NORMAN AUGUSTINE, CEO OF LOCKHEED MARTIN CO.

A mere scholar, a mere ass.

ROBERT BURTON

I'll do anything for money—
even associate with my agent.

VINCENT PRICE

I love deadlines. I especially like the
whooshing sound they make as they go flying by.

DOUGLAS ADAMS, AMERICAN WRITER

Ninety percent of my money I spend on women
and whisky. The rest I just waste.

TUG MCGRAW

I owe the government $3,400 in taxes.
So I sent them two hammers and a toilet seat.

MICHAEL MCSHANE

If I had only known, I would have been a locksmith.

ALBERT EINSTEIN

Education is a wonderful thing. If you couldn't
sign your name you'd have to pay cash.

RITA MAE BROWN

A conference is a gathering of important people
who singly can do nothing, but together can
decide that nothing can be done.

FRED ALLEN

If at first you don't succeed—you're fired.

JEAN GRAMAN

Money couldn't buy friends,
but you get a better class of enemy.

SPIKE MILLIGAN, AMERICAN ACTOR

If at first you don't succeed, you may be
at your level of incompetence already.

LAWRENCE J. PETER

The brain is a wonderful organ. It starts working
the moment you get up in the morning, and does not
stop until you get into the office.

ROBERT FROST

Grad school is the snooze button
on the clock radio of life.

**JOHN ROGERS, COMEDIAN (WHO HOLDS A
GRADUATE DEGREE IN PHYSICS)**

When it's a question of money,
everybody is of the same religion.

VOLTAIRE

Economists are people who work with numbers
but don't have the personality to be accountants.

ANONYMOUS

On my income tax 1040 it says, "Check this box
if you are blind." I wanted to put a check mark
about three inches away.

TOM LEHRER

Never underestimate the effectiveness
of a straight cash bribe.

CLAUDE COCKBURN

Under capitalism man exploits man.
Under communism it's just the opposite.

JOHN KENNETH GALBRAITH

The world is divided into people who do things—
and people who get the credit.

DWIGHT MORROW, AMERICAN LAWYER AND STATESMAN

Beggars should be abolished. It annoys one to
give to them and it annoys one
not to give to them.

FRIEDRICH WILHELM NIETZSCHE (ATTRIBUTED)

Hard work is the soundest investment.
It provides a neat security for your widow's
next husband.

ANONYMOUS

The wit of a graduate student is like champagne.
Canadian champagne.

ROBERTSON DAVIES, CANADIAN WRITER

Economics is extremely useful as
a form of employment for economists.

JOHN KENNETH GALBRAITH

If at first you don't succeed, try, try again.
Then quit. No use being a damn fool about it.

W. C. FIELDS

Money cannot buy health but I'd settle
for a diamond-studded wheelchair.

DOROTHY PARKER

Lottery: A tax on people who are bad at math.

POPULAR BUMPER STICKER

Early to bed and early to rise
usually indicates unskilled labor.

JOHN CIARDI

I wish the banks would just say, "Look you ————,
line up there, we don't give a ———— about your
miserable little bank account."

PAUL FUSSELL

Looking at Clinton's economic program, I feel like a
mosquito in a nudist colony. The real question is
where to strike first.

PHIL GRAMM

The man who writes the bank's advertising slogan
is not the same man who makes the loans.

GEORGE COOTE

One difference between death and taxes is that death doesn't get worse every time Congress meets.

ROY L. SCHAEFER

The cost of living is going up and the chance of living is going down.

FLIP WILSON

I'm a self-made man. Who else would help?

OSCAR LEVANT, AMERICAN ACTOR AND WRITER

I don't want money. It's only people who pay their bills who want money and I never pay mine.

OSCAR WILDE

There are plenty of vacancies, but they're all filled.

CHRISTOPHER RICKS, PROFESSOR,
ON HIS ENGLISH DEPARTMENT

I have enough money to last me the rest of my life, unless I buy something.

JACKIE MASON

Specialists are people who always repeat the same mistakes.

WALTER GROPIUS, GERMAN ARCHITECT

Isn't it strange? The same people who laugh at gypsy fortune tellers take economists seriously.

CINCINNATI ENQUIRER

If someone says, "It's not the money, it's the principle," it's the money.

ANGELO VALENTI

The trick is to stop thinking of it as "your" money.

ANOYMOUS IRS AUDITOR

A billion here, a billion there, and
pretty soon you're talking about real money.

EVERETT DIRKSEN, U.S. SENATOR

The average Ph.D. thesis is nothing
but the transference of bones from
one graveyard to another.

FRANK J. DOBIE, AMERICAN WRITER

If you can count your money,
you don't have a billion dollars.

J. PAUL GETTY

Don't confuse fame with success.
One is Madonna; the other is Helen Keller.

ERMA BOMBECK

Ask five economists and you'll get five different answers (six if one went to Harvard).

 EDGAR R. FIEDLER

I'm proud of paying taxes. The only thing is— I could be just as proud for half the money.

ARTHUR GODFREY

If Karl, instead of writing a lot about capital, had made a lot of it ... it would have been much better.

KARL MARX'S MOTHER

Money isn't everything but it sure keeps you in touch with your children.

J. PAUL GETTY

Today it takes more brains to fill out the income tax
form than it does to make the income.

ALFRED E. NEWMAN

A statistician is someone who is good at figures
but who doesn't have the personality
to be an accountant.

ROY HYDE

The only function of economic forecasting
is to make astrology look respectable.

EZRA SOLOMON

They teach anything in universities today.
You can major in mud pies.

ORSON WELLES

My, my—sixty-five. I guess this marks
the first day of the rest of my life savings.

H. MARTIN

A man must properly pay the fiddler.
In my case it so happened that a whole
symphony orchestra had to be subsidized.

JOHN BARRYMORE, AMERICAN ACTOR

The vanity of teaching often tempts
a man to forget he is a blockhead.

GEORGE SAVILE, LORD HALIFAX

An American is a person who yells for the
government to balance the budget and then
borrows fifty dollars till payday.

H. ALAN DUNN

You show me a capitalist,
I'll show you a bloodsucker.

MALCOLM X

Meetings are an addictive, highly self-indulgent
activity that corporations and other large
organizations habitually engage in only because
they cannot actually masturbate.

DAVE BARRY

The man who leaves money to charity
in his will is merely giving away
what no longer belongs to him.

VOLTAIRE

It takes twenty years to become
an overnight success.

EDDIE CANTOR

They say that money talks, but the only thing
it ever said to me was good-bye.

JOE LOUIS

Being in the Army is like being in the Boy Scouts,
except that the Boy Scouts have adult supervision.

BLAKE CLARK

If something's old and you're trying to sell it,
it's obsolete; if you're trying to buy it,
it's a collector's item.

FRANK ROSS

Anyone can do any amount of work provided
it isn't the work he's supposed to be doing
at the moment.

ROBERT BENCHLEY

A dollar saved is a quarter earned.

JOHN CIARDI

It isn't necessary to be rich and famous to be happy.
It's only necessary to be rich.

ALAN ALDA

If you look up a dictionary of quotations you will
find few reasons for a sensible man to want
to become wealthy.

ROBERT LYND, AMERICAN SOCIOLOGIST

Philanthropist: A rich (and usually bald)
old gentleman who has trained himself to grin
while his conscience is picking his pocket.

AMBROSE BIERCE

Achievement: the death of endeavor
and the birth of disgust.

AMBROSE BIERCE

A charity ball is like a dance except it's
tax deductible.

P. J. O'ROURKE

There is no point at which you can say, "Well,
I'm successful now. I might as well take a nap."

CARRIE FISHER

Lack of money is the root of all evil.

GEORGE BERNARD SHAW

Lots of folks confuse destiny with
bad management.

KIN HUBBARD

Money makes a bastard legitimate.

THE TALMUD

Poor people send their children to school to
be bastards. Rich people teach that at home.

GERALD BARZAN

I like the word *indolence*.
It makes my laziness seem classy.

BERN WILLIAMS

A philanthropist is a man who gives away
what he should be giving back.

ANONYMOUS

It is better to give than to lend,
and it costs about the same.

PHILLIP GIBBS

Basic research is what I'm doing
when I don't know what I'm doing.

WERNER VON BRAUN

I've got all the money I'll ever need
if I die by four o'clock.

HENNY YOUNGMAN

If women can sleep their way to the top, how come
they aren't there? There must be an epidemic of
insomnia out there.

ELLEN GOODMAN

You don't die in the United States,
you underachieve.

JERZY KOZINSKI

I started out with nothing. I still have most of it.

MICHAEL DAVIS, AMERICAN WRITER

There were times when my pants were so thin I could sit on a dime and tell if it was heads or tales.

SPENCER TRACY

I figure you have the same chance of winning the lottery whether you play or not.

FRAN LEBOWITZ, AMERICAN WRITER AND HUMORIST

If I could remember the names of all these particles I'd be a botanist.

ENRICO FERMI

Every day I get up and look through the
Forbes list of the richest people in America.
If I'm not there, I go to work.

ROBERT ORBEN

We trained hard—but it seemed that every time
we were beginning to form up into teams
we were reorganized. I was to learn later in life
that we tend to meet any new situation by
reorganizing, and what a wonderful method
it can be for creating the illusion of progress
while actually producing confusion,
inefficiency, and demoralization.

PETRONIUS ARBITER

CHAPTER 4

HAIL
TO THE
CHIEF

LAW AND JUSTICE,
GOVERNMENT AND POLITICS

Lawyers, I suppose, were children once.

CHARLES LAMB

Freedom of the press is limited
to those who own one.

A. J. LIEBLING

I may not know much, but I know chicken shit
from chicken salad.

LYNDON BAINES JOHNSON

A conservative is one who admires radicals
centuries after they're dead.

LEO C. ROSTEN

There is much to be said for the nouveau riche,
and the Reagans intend to say it all.

GORE VIDAL, ATTRIBUTED

Sometimes at the end of the day when I'm smiling
and shaking hands, I want to kick them.

RICHARD NIXON

Whoever said that talk was cheap
never hired a lawyer.

WAYNE MACKEY

A conservative is a man who is too cowardly
to fight and too fat to run.

ELBERT HUBBARD

If I were two-faced, would I be wearing this one?

ABRAHAM LINCOLN

A government is the only known vessel
that leaks from the top.

JAMES RESTON

The minute you read something you can't understand, you can almost be sure it was written by lawyers.

WILL ROGERS

Jerry Ford is so dumb that he can't fart and chew gum at the same time.

LYNDON BAINES JOHNSON

Asking an incumbent member of Congress to vote for term limits is a bit like asking a chicken to vote for Colonel Sanders.

BOB INGLIS

Government is like a baby: An alimentary canal with a big appetite at one end and no sense of responsibility at the other.

RONALD REAGAN

The modern definition of a *racist* is someone who is winning an argument with a liberal.

PETER BRIMELOW, AMERICAN ECONOMIST AND AUTHOR

We need a president who's fluent in at least one language.

BUCK HENRY, AMERICAN SCREENWRITER

A liberal is man who will give away everything he doesn't own.

FRANK DANE

I either want less corruption, or more chance to participate in it.

ASHLEIGH BRILLIANT, ENGLISH-AMERICAN WRITER

In politics stupidity is not a handicap.

NAPOLEON BONAPARTE

Jimmy Carter is the South's revenge for
Sherman's march through Georgia.

RONALD REAGAN

If God had wanted us to vote,
he would have given us candidates.

JAY LENO

A liberal is a person whose interests
aren't at stake, at the moment.

WILLIS PLAYER

What can you expect from that zoo?

JOHN F. KENNEDY, ON THE U.S. CONGRESS

The great nations have always acted like gangsters,
and the small nations like prostitutes.

STANLEY KUBRICK

Being president is like being a jackass
in a hailstorm. There's nothing to do
but stand there and take it.

LYNDON BAINES JOHNSON

What luck for the rulers that men do not think.

ADOLF HITLER

Juries scare me. I don't want to put my faith
in people who weren't smart enough
to get out of jury duty.

MONICA PIPER

Too bad that all the people
who know how to run the country are busy
driving taxicabs and cutting hair.

GEORGE BURNS

When I was a boy I was told that anybody
could become president; I'm beginning to believe it.

CLARENCE DARROW

The Law, in its majestic equality, forbids the rich,
as well as the poor, to sleep under the bridges,
to beg in the streets, and to steal bread.

ANATOLE FRANCE

How can anyone govern a nation
that has two hundred and forty-six
different kinds of cheese?

CHARLES DE GAULLE

Any society that needs disclaimers
has too many lawyers.

ERIK PEPKE

Politics is for people who have a passion
for changing life but lack a passion for living it.

TOM ROBBINS

Republicans believe every day is the Fourth of July,
but Democrats believe every day is April 15.

RONALD REAGAN

People never lie so much as after a hunt,
during a war, or before an election.

OTTO VON BISMARCK

Man is the only animal that laughs
and has a state legislature.

SAMUEL BUTLER

Everybody has a little bit of Watergate in him.

BILLY GRAHAM

If a tree fell in the forest, and no one was there to hear it, it might sound like Dan Quayle looks.

TOM SHALES, AMERICAN COLUMNIST

The Ten Commandments contain 297 words.
The Bill of Rights is stated in 463 words.
Lincoln's Gettysburg Address contains 266 words.
A recent federal directive to regulate the price
of cabbage contains 26,911 words.

THE ATLANTA JOURNAL

I'd rather have him inside the tent pissing out, than outside the tent pissing in.

LYNDON BAINES JOHNSON, ON KEEPING FBI DIRECTOR J. EDGAR HOOVER

Ignorance of the law must not prevent the lawyer from collecting his fees.

JOHN MORTIMER

My choice early in life was either to be a piano
player in a whorehouse or a politician.
And to tell the truth there's hardly any difference.

HARRY S. TRUMAN

It only takes twenty years for a liberal to become
a conservative without changing a single idea.

ROBERT ANTON WILSON

A jury consists of twelve persons chosen
to decide who has the better lawyer.

ROBERT FROST

The reason there are so few female politicians
is that it is too much trouble to put make-up
on two faces.

MAUREEN MURPHY, COMEDIAN

A town that can't support one lawyer
can always support two.

LYNDON BAINES JOHNSON

The president of today is just
the postage stamp of tomorrow.

GRACIE ALLEN

Conservatives are not necessarily stupid,
but most stupid people are conservatives.

JOHN STUART MILL

I'd rather entrust the government of
the United States to the first 400 people listed
in the Boston telephone directory than to
the faculty of Harvard University.

WILLIAM F. BUCKLEY, JR.

In Washington it is an honor to be disgraced ...
you have to have *been* somebody to fall.

MAX GREENFIELD

I may be president of the United States,
but my private life is nobody's damned business.

CHESTER A. ARTHUR

A liberal is a conservative who's been arrested.
A conservative is a liberal who's been mugged.

VARIOUSLY ATTRIBUTED

A triumph of the embalmer's art.

GORE VIDAL, OF RONALD REAGAN

An ambassador is an honest man sent abroad
to lie for the commonwealth.

SIR HENRY WOTTON

A liberal is a man too broadminded
to take his own side in a quarrel.

ROBERT FROST

If law school is so hard to get through ...
how come there are so many lawyers?

CALVIN TRILLIN

I've been married to one Marxist and one fascist,
and neither one would take the garbage out.

LEE GRANT

The Republicans have a new healthcare proposal:
Just say *no* to illness!

MARK RUSSELL

Rome had senators too, that's why it declined.

FRANK DANE

Where there are two Ph.D.s in a developing country,
one is head of state and the other is in exile.

EDWIN HERBERT SAMUEL

The illegal we do immediately.
The unconstitutional takes a little longer.

HENRY KISSINGER

Candidates should not attempt more than six
of the Ten Commandments.

ROBERT BENCHLEY

The Democrats are the party that says government
will make you smarter, taller, richer, and remove
the crabgrass on your lawn. The Republicans are
the party that says government doesn't work
and then they get elected and prove it.

P. J. O'ROURKE

If the laws could speak for themselves,
they would complain of the lawyers.

SIR GEORGE SAVILLE

My doctor ordered me to shut up,
which will make every American happy.

BILL CLINTON, DURING A BOUT OF LARYNGITIS

It was involuntary. They sank my boat.

JOHN F. KENNEDY, ON HOW HE BECAME A WAR HERO

Satire is alive and well and living
in the White House.

ROBIN WILLIAMS

There ought to be one day—just one—
when there is open season on senators.

WILL ROGERS

This land is your land and this land is
my land—sure—but the world is run
by those that never listen to music anyway.

BOB DYLAN

The vice presidency of the United States
isn't worth a pitcher of warm spit.

JOHN NANCE GARNER

Elections are held to delude the populace into
believing that they are participating in government.

GERALD F. LIEBERMAN

We have to be careful cutting back foreign aid
to third world nations. They need the money,
to buy Soviet weapons.

JOEY ADAMS

Washington is a city of Southern efficiency
and Northern charm.

JOHN F. KENNEDY

Diplomacy is the art of saying "Nice doggie"
until you can find a rock.

WYNN CATLIN

I do not care to speak ill of any man behind
his back but I believe that man is an *attorney*.

SAMUEL JOHNSON

Democracy is an abuse of statistics.

JORGE LUIS BORGES

I think the American public wants a solemn ass as
president and I think I'll go along with them.

CALVIN COOLIDGE

CHAPTER 5

THAT'S ENTERTAINMENT

ARTISTS, ACTORS AND WRITERS, MUSIC, MOVIES, AND TV

Journalism is the only thinkable
alternative to working.

JEFFREY BERNARD

My father hated radio and could not wait for
television to be invented so he could hate that too.

PETER DE VRIES

Show me a poet and I'll show you a shit.

A. J. LIEBLING

You're an actor, are you? Well, all that means is:
you are irresponsible, irrational, romantic, and
incapable of handling an adult emotion or a
universal concept without first reducing it to
something personal, material, sensational—
and probably sexual!

GEORGE HERMAN, PLAYWRIGHT

An editor should have a pimp for a brother,
so he'd have someone to look up to.

GENE FOWLER, AMERICAN DIRECTOR

To save the Theatre, the Theatre must be destroyed,
the actors and actresses all die of the Plague ...
they make art impossible.

ELEANOR DUSE, ITALIAN ACTRESS

All my major works have been written in prison.
I would recommend prison not only to
aspiring writers but to aspiring politicians too.

JAWAHARLAL NEHRU

Shoot a few scenes out of focus. I want you
to win the foreign film award.

BILLY WILDER, TO AN AMERICAN CAMERAMAN

I am sitting in the smallest room in the house.
I have your review in front of me.
Soon it will be behind me.

MAX REGER

Hemingway was a jerk.

HAROLD ROBBINS

I believe in equality for everyone,
except reporters and photographers.

MAHATMA GANDHI

Anyone who can write home for money
can write for magazines.

WILSON MIZNER

This film wasn't released—it escaped.

JAMES CAAN

The only reason I didn't kill myself
after I read the reviews of my first book was
because we have two rivers in New York and
I couldn't decide which one to jump into.

WILFRED SHEED

Today if something is not worth saying,
people sing it.

PIERRE-AUGUSTIN CARON DE BEAUMARCHAIS

People are wrong when they say opera
isn't what it used to be. It is what it used to be—
that's what's wrong with it.

NOËL COWARD

Writing is easy. All you do is stare at a blank sheet
of paper until drops of blood form on your forehead.

GENE FOWLER, AMERICAN DIRECTOR

It's better directing myself than working with
most of the assholes I've made films with.

KLAUS KINSKI

I asked my publisher what would happen
if he sold all the copies of my book he had printed.
He said, "I'll just print another ten."

ERIC SYKES, ENGLISH COMEDIAN

A satire which the censor is able to understand
deserves to be banned.

KARL KRAUS, AUSTRIAN WRITER

Everywhere I go, I am asked if I think the
university stifles writers. My opinion is that
it doesn't stifle enough of them.

FLANNERY O'CONNOR

I've always said there's a place for the press
but they haven't dug it yet.

TOMMY DOCHERTY

All Shakespeare did was string together
a lot of old well-known quotations.

H. L. MENCKEN

If you're going to tell people the truth,
make them laugh, or they'll kill you.

BILLY WILDER

The secret of writing great literature
is to be under house arrest.

GEORG LUKACS

A historian is just an unsuccessful novelist.

H. L. MENCKEN

The dubious privilege of a freelance writer is that he's given the freedom to starve anywhere.

S. J. PERELMAN

Television is the first truly democratic culture—the first culture available to everyone and entirely governed by what the people want. The most terrifying thing is what people *do* want.

CLIVE BARNES, ENGLISH CRITIC

An author is a fool who, not content with having bored those who have lived with him, insists on boring future generations.

CHARLES DE SECONDAT

A satirist is a man who discovers unpleasant things about himself and then says them about other people.

PETER MCARTHUR

Actresses will happen in the best-regulated families.

OLIVER HERFORD, AMERICAN POET

There is no money in poetry,
but there is no poetry in money either.

ROBERT GRAVES

Television? The word is half Greek, half Latin.
No good can come of it.

C. P. SCOTT

I hate authors. I wouldn't mind them so much
if they didn't write books.

POLLY WALKER

Hollywood is a place where you can make
an entire career out of baloney.

WARREN BEATTY

I dreamed the devil appeared the other night
and wanted to bargain for my soul and the
William Morris Agency handled the deal. They got
me damned to hell for eternity—with options.

WOODY ALLEN

Some day I hope to write a book where
the royalties will pay for the copies I give away.

CLARENCE DARROW

People who break their word in Japan
kill themselves. People who break
their word here kill you.

MICHAEL CAINE

Journalism consists in buying white paper at
two cents a pound and selling it at ten cents
a pound.

CHARLES DANA

My agent gets ten percent of everything I get,
except my blinding headaches.

FRED ALLEN

If it's a good script I'll do it. And if it's a bad script,
and they pay me enough, I'll do it.

GEORGE BURNS

An actress is someone with no ability who sits
around waiting to go on alimony.

JACKIE STALLONE

Television is for appearing on, not looking at.

NOËL COWARD

I've known some actors who were intelligent,
but the better the actor, the more stupid he is.

TRUMAN CAPOTE

Women reporters who ask awkward questions
are just trying to prove their manhood.

ROSS PEROT

Working for Warner Brothers is like
fucking a porcupine. It's a hundred pricks
against one.

WILSON MIZNER

I'm just waiting for somebody to say I'm a fag—
that's when you're a really big star!

BURT REYNOLDS

Every good journalist has a novel in him—
which is an excellent place for it.

RUSSELL LYNES

Hollywood is like being nowhere
and talking to nobody about nothing.

MICHELANGELO ANTONIONI

Art is either plagiarism or revolution.

PAUL GAUGUIN

Listening to critics is like letting Muhammad Ali
decide which astronaut goes to the moon.

ROBERT DUVALL

A journalist has no ideas
and the ability to express them.

KARL KRAUS, AUSTRIAN WRITER

Television is democracy at its ugliest.

PADDY CHAYEVSKY, AMERICAN SCREENWRITER

The writing of more than seventy-five poems in a
fiscal year should be punishable by a fine of $500.

ED SANDERS

All television is children's television.

RICHARD P. ADLER

If you can't annoy somebody,
there is little point in writing.

SIR KINGSLEY AMIS

But that's what being an artist is—
feeling crummy before everyone else feels crummy.

THE NEW YORKER

If Botticelli were alive today,
he'd be working for *Vogue*.

PETER USTINOV

Most rock journalism is people who can't write,
interviewing people who can't talk,
for people who can't read.

FRANK ZAPPA

Commercial: The pause that depresses.

ANONYMOUS

Tragedy is when I cut my finger. Comedy is
when you fall into an open sewer and die.

MEL BROOKS

You don't have to be smart to act—look at the
outgoing president of the United States.

CHER

Every asshole has a script in his back pocket.

LARRY COHEN, AMERICAN DIRECTOR

An autobiography is an obituary in serial form
with the last installment missing.

QUENTIN CRISP

If God had an agent, the world wouldn't be
built yet. It'd only be about Thursday.

JERRY REYNOLDS

If my film makes one more person miserable,
I've done my job.

WOODY ALLEN

If it were not for the reporters,
I would tell you the truth.

CHESTER A. ARTHUR

Nothing stinks like a pile of unpublished writing.

SYLVIA PLATH

Over in Hollywood they almost made a
great picture, but they caught it in time.

WILSON MIZNER

I don't know anything about music.
In my line you don't have to.

ELVIS PRESLEY

Nobody is worth what they pay me.

BURT REYNOLDS

I don't own any of my own paintings because
a Picasso original costs several thousand dollars
and that's a luxury I can't afford.

PABLO PICASSO

No author is a man of genius to his publisher.

HEINRICH HEINE

Television enables you to be entertained
in your home by people you wouldn't have
in your home.

DAVID FROST, ENGLISH TALK-SHOW HOST

Art is a collaboration between God and the artist,
and the less the artist does the better.

ANDRÉ GIDE

Dealing with network executives is like
being nibbled to death by ducks.

ERIC SEVAREID

A best-seller is the gilded tomb
of a mediocre talent.

LOGAN PEARSAL SMITH

A director must be a policeman, a midwife,
a psychoanalyst, a sycophant, and a bastard.

BILLY WILDER

There are three kinds of lies:
lies, damned lies, and statistics.

BENJAMIN DISRAELI

I'm a lousy writer; a helluva lot of people
have got lousy taste.

GRACE MATALIOUS

Asking a working writer what he thinks
about critics is like asking a lamppost
how it feels about dogs.

CHRISTOPHER HAMPTON

The dead actor requested in his will that
his body be cremated and ten percent of his ashes
thrown in his agent's face.

ANONYMOUS

Suicide attempts and then writing poems
about your suicide attempts is just pure bullshit.

PHILIP LARKIN

It is one of the tragic ironies of the theater
that only one man in it can count on steady work—
the night watchman.

TALLULAH BANKHEAD

If a young writer can refrain from writing,
he shouldn't hesitate to do so.

ANDRÉ GIDE

One of the signs of Napoleon's greatness
is the fact that he once had a publisher shot.

SIEGFRIED UNSELD

It is said that life begins when the fetus can exist
apart from its mother. By this definition, many
people in Hollywood are legally dead.

JAY LENO

I think Shakespeare is shit! Absolute shit!
He may have been a genius for his time,
but I just can't relate to that stuff. "Thee" and
"Thou"—the guy sounds like a faggot.

GENE SIMMONS

Television is more interesting than people.
If it were not, we would have people standing
in the corners of our rooms.

ALAN CORENK

I do not think Rousseau's poem "Ode to Posterity"
will reach its destination.

VOLTAIRE

Only in show business could a guy with a
C-minus average be considered an intellectual.

MORT SAHL

Hell is a half-filled auditorium.

ROBERT FROST

You ask if I keep a copy of every book I print.
Madam, I keep thousands.

JONATHAN CAPE

Bad artists always admire each other's work.

OSCAR WILDE

Poetry is nobody's business except the poet's, and everybody else can fuck off.

PHILLIP LARKIN

Right now I'm the greatest. I don't say this out of vanity—it's just that the rest are so bad.

SALVADOR DALÍ

Studying literature at Harvard is like learning about women at the Mayo Clinic.

ROY BLOUNT, JR.

Publishing a volume of poetry today is like dropping a rose petal down the Grand Canyon and waiting for the echo.

DON MARQUIS

A good many young writers make the mistake
of enclosing a stamped, self-addressed envelope,
big enough for the manuscript to come back in.
This is too much of a temptation for the editor.

RING LARDNER

If more than ten percent of the population likes
a painting, it should be burned, for it must be bad.

GEORGE BERNARD SHAW

Skill without imagination is craftsmanship
and gives us many useful objects such as
wickerwork picnic baskets. Imagination
without skill gives us modern art.

TOM STOPPARD

My collected works are mostly on the vomit bags
of Pan American and TWA.

CHARLES MCCABE

Sculpture: mud pies which endure.

CYRIL CONNOLLY, ENGLISH CRITIC

The poet ranks far below the painter in the representation of visible things, and far below the musician in that of invisible things.

LEONARDO DA VINCI

For half a century, photography has been the art form of the untalented.

GORE VIDAL

Abstract art: a product of the untalented sold by the unprincipled to the utterly bewildered.

AL CAPP

You have Van Gogh's ear for music.

BILLY WILDER

A typical day in the life of a heavy metal musician consists of a round of golf and an AA meeting.

BILLY JOEL

It's not so much that I write well, I just don't write badly very often, and that passes for good on television.

ANDY ROONEY

A novel is a prose narrative of some length that has something wrong with it.

RANDALL JARRELL (ATTRIBUTED)

Critics can't even make music by rubbing their back legs together.

MEL BROOKS

The importance of a public speaker bears
an inverse relationship to the number of
microphones into which he speaks.

WILLIAM MORGAN

Journalist: a person without any ideas but with
an ability to express them; a writer whose skill
is improved by a deadline: the more time he has,
the worse he writes.

KARL KRAUS

In Hollywood, writers are considered
only the first drafts of human beings.

FRANK DEFORD, SPORTSWRITER

It takes the publishing industry so long to produce
books it's no wonder so many are posthumous.

TERESSA SKELTON

Acting has been described as
farting about in disguise.

PETER O'TOOLE

Radio news is bearable. This is due to the fact
that while the news is being broadcast
the disc jockey is not allowed to talk.

FRAN LEBOWITZ, AMERICAN WRITER AND HUMORIST

Do you know what the best three years of
a sportswriter's life are?
Third grade.

GEORGE RAVELING

CHAPTER 6

MEN AND WOMEN, LOVE AND MARRIAGE,
ROMANCE AND SEX

When God created two sexes, he may have been overdoing it.

VARIOUSLY ATTRIBUTED

I couldn't see tying myself down to a middle-aged woman with four children, even though the woman was my wife and the children were my own.

JOSEPH HELLER

Women love cats. Men say they love cats, but when women aren't looking, men kick cats.

MATT GROENING

Men have a much better time of it than women. For one thing, they marry later; for another thing, they die earlier.

H. L. MENCKEN

I'd like to get married because I like the idea
of a man being required by law to
sleep with me every night.

CARRIE SNOW, COMEDIAN

The trouble in the world is nearly all due to the fact
that one half the people are men,
and the other half, women.

EDGAR WATSON HOWE, AMERICAN WRITER AND EDITOR

The main difference between men and women
is that men are lunatics and women are idiots.

REBECCA WEST, IRISH AUTHOR AND JOURNALIST

I was married by a judge.
I should have asked for a jury.

GEORGE BURNS

Boy Meets Girl, So What?

BERTOLT BRECHT

For a single woman, preparing for company
means wiping the lipstick off the milk carton.

ELAYNE BOOSLER, COMEDIAN

I heard a man say that brigands demand your
money or your life, whereas women require both.

SAMUEL BUTLER, ENGLISH NOVELIST

How much fame, money, and power
does a woman have to achieve on her own
before you can punch her in the face?

P. J. O'ROURKE

Marriage has driven more than one man to sex.

PETER DE VRIES, AMERICAN AUTHOR AND HUMORIST

I hated my marriage, but I always
had a great place to park.

GERALD NACHMAN, AUTHOR

Women give us solace, but if it were not
for women we should never need solace.

DON HEROLD, AMERICAN AUTHOR AND HUMORIST

In my youth there were words you couldn't say
in front of a girl; now you can't say *girl*.

TOM LEHRER

If I ever marry it will be on a sudden impulse,
as a man shoots himself.

H. L. MENCKEN

Monogamy: a synonym for monotony.

GREGORY NUNN

The ten best years of a woman's life
are between twenty-nine and thirty.

PETER WEISS, GERMAN DRAMATIST

My wife doesn't care what I do while I'm away
as long as I don't have a good time.

LEE TREVINO

The only trouble with sexually liberating women
is that there aren't enough sexually liberated men
to go around.

GLORIA STEINEM

My wife and I tried to breakfast together,
but we had to stop or our marriage
would have been wrecked.

WINSTON CHURCHILL

The difference between divorce and legal separation
is that a legal separation gives a husband time
to hide his money.

JOHNNY CARSON

Once I tried to explain to a fellow feminist
why I liked wearing makeup: she replied by
explaining why she does not. Neither of us
understood a word the other said.

NORA EPHRON, AMERICAN AUTHOR AND SCREENWRITER

When I go to the beauty parlor,
I always use the emergency entrance.

PHYLLIS DILLER

You'd be surprised how much it costs
to look this cheap.

DOLLY PARTON

Bigamy is having one husband too many.
Monogamy is the same.

ERICA JONG

A woman without a man
is like a fish without a bicycle.

GLORIA STEINEM (ATTRIBUTED)

Ms. – a syllable which sounds like a
bumblebee breaking wind.

HORTENSE CALISHER, WRITER

Behind every successful man
stands a surprised mother-in-law.

HUBERT HUMPHREY

I base my fashion sense on what doesn't itch.

GILDA RADNER

Social progress can be measured exactly
by the social position of the fair sex—
the ugly ones included.

KARL MARX

The vote, I thought, means nothing to women.
We should be armed.

EDNA O'BRIEN, IRISH WRITER AND PACIFIST

Marriage is a wonderful invention;
but then again so is a bicycle repair kit.

BILLY CONNOLLY, ENGLISH COMEDIAN

If beauty is truth, why don't women
go to the library to have their hair done?

LILY TOMLIN

Take it from me, marriage isn't a word …
it's a sentence!

VARIOUSLY ATTRIBUTED

I don't see many men today. I see a lot of guys
running around television with small waists,
but I don't see many men.

ANTHONY QUINN

The claim that American women are downtrodden
and unfairly treated is the fraud of the century.

PHYLLIS SCHLAFLY

The only time some fellows are seen with their wives
is after they've been indicted.

KIN HUBBARD, AMERICAN JOURNALIST AND HUMORIST

It takes a woman twenty years to make a man of her son, and another woman twenty minutes to make a fool of him.

HELEN ROWLAND, IRISH-AMERICAN WRITER

It wasn't exactly a divorce—I was traded.

TIM CONWAY

Men adore women. Our mothers taught us to. Women do not adore men; women are amused by men, we are a source of chuckles.

GARRISON KEILLOR

I belong to Bridegrooms Anonymous. Whenever I feel like getting married, they send over a lady in a housecoat and hair curlers to burn my toast for me.

DICK MARTIN

When you go to drown yourself, take off
your clothes. They may fit your wife's next husband.

GREGORY NUNN

A woman never sees what we do for her;
she only sees what we don't do.

GEORGES COURTELINE, FRENCH HUMORIST

They came out with a new perfume that's bound
to be a sure hit with men. It smells like beer.

SUSAN SAVANNAH, AMERICAN HUMORIST

Okay, so maybe I am saying guys are scum.
But they're not mean-spirited scum. And few
of them—even when they are out of town
on business trips and have a clear-cut
opportunity—will poop on the floor.

DAVE BARRY

The chief excitement in a woman's life
is spotting women fatter than she is.

HELEN ROWLAND, IRISH-AMERICAN WRITER

Of the seven dwarves, only Dopey
had a shaven face. This should tell us something
about the custom of shaving.

TOM ROBBINS

A husband should not insult his wife publicly,
at parties. He should insult her in the privacy
of the home.

JAMES THURBER

Some men are so macho they'll get you pregnant
just to kill a rabbit.

MAUREEN MURPHY, COMEDIAN

Women speak because they wish to speak,
whereas a man speaks only when driven
to speech by something outside himself, like,
for instance, he can't find any clean socks.

JEAN KERR, AMERICAN WRITER AND HUMORIST

My wife's jealousy is getting ridiculous.
The other day she looked at my calendar
and wanted to know who May was.

RODNEY DANGERFIELD

Educating a woman is like pouring honey
into a fine Swiss watch: everything stops.

KURT VONNEGUT

Probably the only place where a man can feel
really secure is in a maximum-security prison,
except for the imminent threat of release.

GERMAINE GREER, ENGLISH REFORMER AND WRITER

If they can put one man on the moon,
why can't they put them all there?

VARIOUSLY ATTRIBUTED

I'd marry again if I found a man
who had fifteen million dollars, would sign over
half of it to me before the marriage,
and guarantee he'd be dead within a year.

BETTE DAVIS

Alimony: Disinterest, compounded annually.

WALTER MCDONALD, AMERICAN POET

Many a man owes his success to his first wife
and his second wife to his success.

JIM BACKUS

No nice men are good at getting taxis.

KATHERINE WHITEHORN, ENGLISH WRITER

Men do not settle down. Men surrender.

CHRIS ROCK

If men could get pregnant,
abortion would be a sacrament.

FLORYNCE KENNEDY, AMERICAN FEMINIST AND WRITER

I know a mother-in-law who sleeps with her
glasses on, the better to see her son-in-law
suffer in her dreams.

ERNEST COQUELIN, FRENCH COMIC ACTOR

A man running after a hat is not half so ridiculous
as a man running after a woman.

G. K. CHESTERTON

After seven years of marriage, I'm sure of two things. First, never wallpaper together, and second, you'll need two bathrooms. Both for her.

DENNIS MILLER

Marriage is grounds for divorce.

ANONYMOUS

Strange to say what delight we married people have to see these poor people decoyed into our condition.

SAMUEL PEPYS

Show me a man who lives alone and has a perpetually clean kitchen, and eight times out of nine, I'll show you a man with detestable spiritual qualities.

CHARLES BUKOWSKI, AMERICAN AUTHOR

A lot of people have asked me how short I am.
Since my last divorce, I think I'm about
$100,000 short.

MICKEY ROONEY

I've always held that a bachelor is a fellow
who never makes the same mistake once.

GARY COOPER, IN *NORTHWEST MOUNTED POLICE*

The only good husbands stay bachelors;
they're too considerate to get married.

FINLEY PETER DUNNE, AMERICAN JOURNALIST AND HUMORIST

If you want to find out some things
about yourself—and in vivid detail, too—
just try calling your wife "fat."

P. J. O'ROURKE

By all means marry: if you get a good wife
you'll become happy; if you get a bad one,
you'll become a philosopher.

SOCRATES

A bachelor is a man who is right sometimes.

ANONYMOUS

In Biblical times, a man could have as many wives
as he could afford. Just like today.

ABIGAIL VAN BUREN (DEAR ABBY)

Because sex on the first date, or sooner if possible,
is his goal, does not mean that the man feels he owes
the woman anything. In fact, if she succumbs too
quickly, she might lose her chance at the movie
(unless the movie involves some kind of martial
arts, since he was definitely going to see it anyway).

MERRILL MARKOE, AUTHOR

However much you dislike your mother-in-law
you must not set fire to her.

ERNEST WILD

If you are living with a man, you don't have
to worry about whether you should
sleep with him after dinner.

STEPHANIE BRUSH, HUMORIST AND COLUMNIST

With the catching end the pleasures of the chase.

ABRAHAM LINCOLN

Half of all marriages end in divorce—
and then there are the real unhappy ones.

JOAN RIVERS

My wife doesn't. Understand me?

WILLIAM COLE

If you never want to see a man again, say "I love you. I want to marry you. I want to have children"—they leave skid marks.

RITA RUDNER, AMERICAN COMEDIAN

Bigamy is having one wife too many. Monogamy is the same.

OSCAR WILDE

When you're in a relationship, you're always surrounded by a ring of circumstances ... joined together by a wedding ring, or in a boxing ring.

BOB SEGER

If you are looking for a kindly, well-to-do older gentleman who is no longer interested in sex, take out an ad in the *Wall Street Journal*.

ABIGAIL VAN BUREN (DEAR ABBY)

Early to bed and early to rise,
and your girl will go out with other guys.

ANONYMOUS

Alimony: The cash surrender value
of the American Male.

ANONYMOUS

A relationship is what happens between
two people who are waiting for something better
to come along.

ANONYMOUS

My divorce came as a complete surprise to me.
This will happen when you haven't been home
in eighteen years.

LEE TREVINO

Never date a woman you can hear ticking.

MARK PATINKIN, COLUMNIST

A wife is a person who reminds you that her
allowance is not as big as her alimony would be.

VAUGHN MONROE, AMERICAN BANDLEADER

Dating: Finding someone
so you won't have to date again.

SUSAN ST. JAMES

Friendship among women is only
a suspension of hostilities.

ANTOINE DE RIVAROL, FRENCH JOURNALIST

The prostitute is the only honest woman
left in America.

TI-GRACE ATKINSON, AMERICAN FEMINIST

The perfect lover is one who
turns into a pizza at 4:00 A.M.

CHARLES PIERCE, AMERICAN FEMALE IMPERSONATOR

Personally, I think if a woman hasn't met the right
man by the time she's 24, she may be lucky.

JEAN KERR, AMERICAN AUTHOR AND HUMORIST

When I have to cry, I think about my love life.
When I have to laugh, I think about my love life.

GLENDA JACKSON

Dating is always a problem for women.
The man who looks as if he may be
a good husband probably is.

ANONYMOUS

If you feel like getting a divorce, you are no exception to the general rule.

ELIZABETH HAWES, AUTHOR

If the right man does not come along, there are many fates far worse. One is to have the wrong man come along.

LETITIA BALDRIDGE, ETIQUETTE COLUMNIST

I have such poor vision I can date anybody.

GARRY SHANDLING

Whenever I want a really nice meal, I start dating again.

SUSAN HEALY, COMEDIAN

I was married once. Now I just lease.

FROM THE FILM *BUDDY, BUDDY*

LADY ASTOR: If you were my husband, Winston, I'd put poison in your tea.

WINSTON CHURCHILL: If I were your husband, Nancy, I'd drink it.

I can't get a relationship to last longer than it takes to make copies of their tapes.

MARGARET SMITH, WRITER AND COMEDIAN

How many of you have ever started dating because you were too lazy to commit suicide?

JUDY TENUTA

Love is the delightful interval between meeting a beautiful girl and discovering that she looks like a haddock.

JOHN BARRYMORE, AMERICAN ACTOR

The trouble with my wife is that she's a
whore in the kitchen and a cook in bed.

GEOFFREY GORER, ENGLISH WRITER AND ANTHROPOLOGIST

A psychiatrist asks a lot of expensive questions
your wife asks for nothing.

JOEY ADAMS, HUMORIST

Ah, love—the walks over soft grass,
the smiles over candlelight, the arguments
over just about everything else.

MAX HEADROOM

Love is just a system for getting someone
to call you darling after sex.

JULIAN BARNES, ENGLISH NOVELIST

My first wife divorced me on grounds of
incompatibility—and besides, I think she hated me.

OSCAR LEVANT, AMERICAN ACTOR AND WRITER

Love is a snowmobile racing across the tundra
and then suddenly it flips over, pinning
you underneath. At night, the ice weasels come.

MATT GROENING

Love is what you feel for a dog or a pussycat.
It doesn't apply to humans.

JOHNNY ROTTEN

I've married a few people I shouldn't have,
but haven't we all?

MAMIE VAN DOREN, AMERICAN ACTRESS

When people say, "You're breaking my heart,"
they do in fact usually mean that you're
breaking their genitals.

JEFFREY BERNARD, ENGLISH COLUMNIST

Who would have ever thought you could die
from sex? It was much more fun
when you only went to hell.

JOHN WATERS, AMERICAN FILMMAKER

Marie Osmond makes Mother Teresa
look like a slut.

JOAN RIVERS

The majority of husbands remind me of
an orangutan trying to play the violin.

HONORÉ DE BALZAC

When a man opens the car door for his wife,
it's either a new car or a new wife.

PRINCE PHILLIP, DUKE OF EDINBURGH

I can remember when the air was clean
and sex was dirty.

GEORGE BURNS

There are a number of mechanical devices
which increase sexual arousal, particularly
in women. Chief among these is the
Mercedes-Benz 380SL convertible.

P. J. O'ROURKE

I remember after I got that marriage license
I went across from the license bureau to a bar for
a drink. The bartender said, "What'll you have, sir?"
And I said, "A glass of hemlock."

ERNEST HEMINGWAY

Marriage is like a bank account. You put it in, you take it out, you lose interest.

VARIOUSLY ATTRIBUTED

I have a self-esteem problem. During sex I fantasize that I'm someone else.

RICHARD LEWIS, COMEDIAN

For birth control I rely on my own personality.

MILT ABEL, AMERICAN COMEDIAN

Condoms aren't completely safe. A friend of mine was wearing one and got hit by a bus.

BOB RUBIN, AMERICAN COMEDIAN AND WRITER

I believe that sex is one of the most beautiful, natural, wholesome things that money can buy.

STEVE MARTIN

There's nothing better than good sex. But bad sex?
A peanut butter and jelly sandwich
is better than bad sex.

BILLY JOEL

I don't think I'll ever get remarried, I'll just find
a woman I don't like and give her a house.

LEWIS GRIZZARD

Many a good hanging prevents a bad marriage.

WILLIAM SHAKESPEARE

Any good whore knows more about sex
than Betty Friedan.

SAM PECKINPAH, AMERICAN FILM DIRECTOR

[Sex is] the last important human activity
not subject to taxation.

RUSSELL BAKER

The most difficult year of marriage
is the one you're in.

FRANKLIN P. JONES, AMERICAN BUSINESSMAN

Anyone who eats three meals a day
should understand why cookbooks
outsell sex books three to one.

L. M. BOYD

I think there are two areas where new ideas
are terribly dangerous—economics and sex.
By and large, it's all been tried before, and if
it's new, it's probably illegal or unhealthy.

FELIX ROHATYN, AMERICAN BUSINESSMAN

Eighty percent of married men cheat in America.
The rest cheat in Europe.

JACKIE MASON

Literature is mostly about sex and not much
about having children and life is
the other way around.

DAVID LODGE

The first part of our marriage was very happy.
But then, on the way back from the ceremony ...

HENNY YOUNGMAN

Leaving sex to the feminists is like letting
your dog vacation at the taxidermist.

CAMILLE PAGLIA

Married. It was like a dream come true for Donna. Just think, soon her little girl would have unpaid bills, unplanned babies, calls from the bank, and substandard housing. All the things a mother dreams of for her child.

ERMA BOMBECK

All men make mistakes, but married men find out about them sooner.

RED SKELTON

A man can have two, maybe three love affairs while he's married. After that it's cheating.

YVES MONTAND

A hundred years ago Hester Prynne of *The Scarlet Letter* was given an A for Adultery; today she would rate no better than a C-plus.

PETER DE VRIES, AMERICAN AUTHOR AND HUMORIST

CHAPTER 7

FAMILY AND CHILDREN

A pregnant woman wants toasted snow.

HEBREW PROVERB

All God's children are not beautiful.
Most of God's children are, in fact,
barely presentable.

FRAN LEBOWITZ, AMERICAN WRITER AND HUMORIST

Some families have skeletons in the closet—
with us the skeletons have the run of the house
and we live in the closet.

JOE McCARROLL

The most effective form of birth control I know
is spending a day with my kids.

JILL BENSLY

I'm absolutely sure there is no life on Mars.
It's not listed on my daughter's phone bills.

LARRY MATTHEWS, AMERICAN JOURNALIST

My biological clock is ticking so loudly I'm nearly
deafened by it. They search me going into planes.

MARIAN KEYES, IRISH NOVELIST

Having a baby is like taking your lower lip
and forcing it over your head.

CAROL BURNETT

The fundamental defect of fathers is that they
want their children to be a credit to them.

BERTRAND RUSSELL, ENGLISH PHILOSOPHER
AND MATHEMATICIAN

My children weary me. I can only see them
as defective adults; feckless, destructive,
frivolous, sensual, humorless.

EVELYN WAUGH

Never raise your hand to your children—
it leaves your midsection unprotected.

ROBERT ORBEN

Boys will be boys—and so will
a lot of middle-aged men.

KIN HUBBARD, AMERICAN JOURNALIST AND HUMORIST

One of the disadvantages of having children
is that they eventually get old enough
to give you presents they make at school.

ROBERT BYRNE

I am fond of children—except boys.

LEWIS CARROLL

Father's Day is like Mother's Day,
except the gift is cheaper.

COLIN BOWLES

Happiness is having a large, loving, caring,
closeknit family in another city.

GEORGE BURNS

My grandfather used to make home movies
and edit out the joy.

RICHARD LEWIS

Sometimes when I look at all my children, I say
to myself, "Lillian, you should have stayed a virgin."

LILLIAN CARTER

Be tolerant of the human race. Your whole
family belongs to it—and some of your
spouse's family does too.

ANONYMOUS

Children today are tyrants. They contradict
their parents, gobble their food,
and tyrannize their teachers.

SOCRATES

I figure if my kids are alive at the end of the day,
I've done my job.

ROSEANNE

The luckiest man in the world was Adam—
he had no mother-in-law.

SHOLOM ALEICHEM

Women who emasculate are called "mothers."

ABIGAIL VAN BUREN (DEAR ABBY)

As a teenager you are in the last stage of life when you will be happy to hear that the phone is for you.

FRAN LEBOWITZ, AMERICAN WRITER AND HUMORIST

My family was so poor the lady next door gave birth to me.

LEE TREVINO

When they come up with a riding vacuum cleaner, then I'll clean the house.

ROSEANNE

Suicide is belated acquiescence to the opinion of one's wife's relatives.

H. L. MENCKEN

If pregnancy were a book
they would cut the last two chapters.

NORA EPHRON, AMERICAN AUTHOR AND SCREENWRITER

No matter how old a mother is she watches her
middle-aged children for signs of improvement.

FLORIDA SCOTT-MAXWELL, AMERICAN WRITER

They fuck you up, your mum and dad.
They may not mean to, but they do
They fill you with the faults they had
And add some extra just for you.

PHILIP LARKIN

Why not give your son a motorcycle
for his last birthday?

COLIN BOWLES

Children are a torment and nothing else.

LEO TOLSTOY

Homosexuality is God's way of ensuring that
the truly gifted are not burdened with children.

SAM AUSTIN

Do not join encounter groups. If you enjoy
being made to feel inadequate, call your mother.

LIZ SMITH

Children are nature's very own
form of birth control.

DAVE BARRY

My father died when I was eight.
At least that's what he told us in the letter.

DREW CAREY

I take my children everywhere but they always
find their way home again.

ROBERT ORBEN

There's nothing wrong with teenagers
that reasoning with them won't aggravate.

JEAN KERR

I love children, especially when they cry,
for then someone takes them away.

NANCY MITFORD

The childless escape much misery.

EURIPEDES

Having a family is like having a bowling alley
installed in your brain.

MARTIN MULL

Somewhere on this globe, every ten seconds,
there is a woman giving birth to a child.
She must be found and stopped.

SAM LEVENSON, AMERICAN HUMORIST

Boys are beyond the range of anybody's sure
understanding, at least when they are between
the ages of eighteen months and ninety years.

JAMES THURBER

CHAPTER 8

THE MAD, MAD WORLD

PEOPLE AND PLACES, CIVILIZATION AND
TECHNOLOGY, HISTORY AND CULTURE

Hell is other people.

JEAN-PAUL SARTRE

The United States is like the guy at the party
who gives cocaine to everybody
and still nobody likes him.

JIM SAMUELS

I wonder if anybody ever reached the age
of thirty-five in New England without wanting
to kill himself.

BARRETT WENDELL

Few people can be happy unless they hate
some other person, nation, or creed.

BERTRAND RUSSELL, ENGLISH PHILOSOPHER
AND MATHEMATICIAN

Science may carry us to Mars, but it will leave
the world peopled as ever by the inept.

AGNES REPPLIER

Thanks to the interstate highway system,
it is now possible to travel across the country
from coast to coast without seeing anything.

CHARLES KURALT

New York Taxi Rules:
1. Driver speaks no English.
2. Driver just got here two days ago from
   someplace like Senegal.
3. Driver hates you.

DAVE BARRY

The trouble with the world is that it's always
one drink behind.

HUMPHREY BOGART

Is it progress if a cannibal uses a knife and fork?

STANISLAW LEM, POLISH WRITER

The goddamn human race deserves itself,
and as far as I'm concerned it can have it.

ELIZABETH JANEWAY

All phone calls are obscene.

KAREN ELIZABETH GORDON

I hate small towns because once you've seen
the cannon in the park, there's nothing else to do.

LENNY BRUCE

In England there are sixty different religions
and only one sauce.

FRANCESCO CARACCIOLO

What a pity, when Christopher Columbus
discovered America, that he never mentioned it.

MARGOT ASQUITH

Some people are so sensitive they feel snubbed
if an epidemic overlooks them.

KIN HUBBARD

A flaw in the human character is that
everyone wants to build and no one
wants to do maintenance.

KURT VONNEGUT

I moved to New York City for my health.
I'm paranoid and it was the only place
where my fears were justified.

ANITA WEISS

Nothing is wrong with southern California that
a rise in the ocean level wouldn't cure.

ROSS MACDONALD

I am willing to love all mankind,
except for an American.

SAMUEL JOHNSON

Progress might have been all right once,
but it's gone on too long.

OGDEN NASH

With friends like you, who needs enemas?

MATTHEW BRODERICK

What can you say about a society that says
God is dead and Elvis is alive?

IRV KUPCINET

I had always loved beautiful and artistic things,
though before leaving America I had had
a very little chance of seeing any.

DAME EMMA ALBANI, CANADIAN OPERA SINGER

Prediction is very difficult,
especially about the future.

NIELS BOHR, PHYSICIST

I have found little that is good about human beings.
In my experience most of them,
on the whole, are trash.

SIGMUND FREUD

Traffic signals in New York
are just rough guidelines.

DAVID LETTERMAN

If you want a picture of the future, imagine a
boot stomping on a human face—forever.

GEORGE ORWELL

The average person thinks he isn't.

LARRY LORENZONI

History is more or less bunk.

HENRY FORD

The only interesting thing that can happen
in a Swiss bedroom is suffocation
by a feather mattress.

ANONYMOUS

When people are free to do what they please,
they usually imitate each other.

ERIC HOFFER

Change of weather is the discourse of fools.

THOMAS FULLER

The U.S. is the only country where failure to promote yourself is widely considered arrogant.

GARRY TRUDEAU

Miami Beach is where neon goes to die.

LENNY BRUCE

I have been trying all my life to like Scotchmen, and am obliged to desist from the experiment in despair.

CHARLES LAMB

Outer space is no place for a person of breeding.

LADY VIOLET BONHAM CARTER

New York is a catastrophe—
but a magnificent catastrophe.

CHARLES-EDWARD LE CORBUSIER, FRENCH ARCHITECT

If it is true we have sprung from the ape,
there are occasions when my own spring
appears not to have been very far.

CORNELIA OTIS SKINNER

I am becoming a socialist. I love humanity,
but I hate people.

EDNA ST. VINCENT MILLAY

History: an account mostly false, of events
unimportant, which are brought about by rulers
mostly knaves, and soldiers mostly fools.

AMBROSE BIERCE

Society is a hospital of incurables.

RALPH WALDO EMERSON

Boston's freeway system was clearly designed by a person who had spent his entire life crashing trains.

BILL BRYSON

History will be kind to me for I intend to write it.

WINSTON CHURCHILL

[Houston] has been an act of real estate rather than an act of God or man.

ADA LOUISE HUXTABLE

We owe to the Middle Ages the worst two inventions of Humanity—romantic love and gun powder.

ANDRÉ MAUROIS

I come from Indiana, the home of more first-rate second-class men than any state in the union.

THOMAS R. MARSHALL (ATTRIBUTED)

Technology ... the knack of so arranging the world that we need not experience it.

BERTOLT BRECHT

The principal difference between the husbandryman and the historian is that the former breeds sheep or cows or such, and the latter breeds (assumed) facts. The husbandryman uses his skills to enrich the future; the historian uses his to enrich the past. Both are usually up to their ankles in bullshit.

TOM ROBBINS

If I owned Hell and Texas,
I'd rent out Texas and live in Hell.

GENERAL PHILIP H. SHERIDAN

Any event, once it has occurred, can be made
to appear inevitable by a competent historian.

LEE SIMONSON

I reckon no man is thoroughly miserable
until he be condemned to live in Ireland.

JONATHAN SWIFT

To err is human but to really foul things up
requires a computer.

ANONYMOUS

Abandon it.

FRANK LLOYD WRIGHT, ON PITTSBURGH, PENNSYLVANIA

Love your enemies in case your friends
turn out to be a bunch of bastards.

R. A. DICKINSON

A narcissist is someone better looking than you are.

GORE VIDAL

What is history but a fable agreed upon?

NAPOLEON BONAPARTE

People shouldn't be treated like objects.
They're not that valuable.

P. J. O'ROURKE

I have received no more than one or two letters
in my life that were worth the postage.

HENRY DAVID THOREAU

Fall is my favorite season in Los Angeles, watching the birds change color and fall from the trees.

DAVID LETTERMAN

We seem to have a compulsion these days to bury time capsules in order to give those people living in the next century or so some idea of what we are like. I have prepared one of my own. I have placed some rather large samples of dynamite, gunpowder, and nitroglycerin. My time capsule is set to go off in the year 3000. It will show them what we are really like.

ALFRED HITCHCOCK

The English think incompetence is the same thing as insincerity.

QUENTIN CRISP

It is not a fragrant world.

RAYMOND CHANDLER

Privacy—you can't find it anywhere,
not even if you want to hang yourself.

MENANDER, GREEK POET AND PLAYWRIGHT

What we call progress is the exchange
of one nuisance for another.

HAVELOCK ELLIS

I have seen the future America
and it does not work.

PHILIP TOYNBEE

The automobile changed our dress, manners,
social customs, vacation habits, the shape of our
cities, consumer purchasing patterns,
common tastes, and positions in intercourse.

JOHN KEATS

Energy experts have announced the development
of a new fuel made from human brain tissue.
It's called assohol.

GEORGE CARLIN

France is a country where the money falls apart
and you can't tear the toilet paper.

BILLY WILDER

Unquestionably, there is progress. The average
American now pays out twice as much in taxes
as he formerly got in wages.

H. L. MENCKEN

Yesterday a bum asked me if I could spare $2.75
for a double cappuccino with no foam.

BILL JONES

Perhaps the only true dignity of man
is his capacity to despise himself.

GEORGE SANTAYANA

If you want to eat well in England,
eat three breakfasts.

W. SOMERSET MAUGHAM

Edison did not invent the first talking machine.
He invented the first one that could be turned off.

ANONYMOUS

Fish and guests smell after three days.

BENJAMIN FRANKLIN

No one ever went broke underestimating
the taste of the American public.

H. L. MENCKEN

New York now leads the world's great cities in the number of people around whom you shouldn't make a sudden move.

DAVID LETTERMAN

Some scientists claim that hydrogen, because it is so plentiful, is the basic building block of the universe. I dispute that. I say that there is more stupidity than hydrogen, and that is the basic building block of the universe.

FRANK ZAPPA

Insect repellent is just one of a number of joke items available in any chemist shop.

HENRY BEARD

The world just doesn't work. it's an idea whose time is gone.

JOSEPH HELLER

Show a Welshman 1,001 exits, one of which is
marked "self destruction" and he'll go
right through that one.

JOSEPH L. MANKIEWICZ

For a list of all the ways technology has failed
to improve the quality of life, please press three.

ALICE KAHN

The freeway is ... the place where Angelinos
spend the two calmest and rewarding hours
of their daily lives.

RAYNAR BANHAM

Any time you see a Hungarian, kick him.
He'll know why.

ANONYMOUS

The world is disgracefully managed,
one hardly knows to whom to complain.

RONALD FIRBANK, ENGLISH NOVELIST

Belgium is a country invented by the British
to annoy the French.

CHARLES DE GAULLE

Making duplicate copies and computer printouts
of things no one wanted even one of in the first
place is giving America a new sense of purpose.

ROBERT CRINGELY, TECHNOLOGY WRITER

America is the only nation in history
which miraculously has gone directly from
barbarism to degeneration without the
usual intervention of civilization.

GEORGES CLEMENCEAU

Culture is an instrument wielded by professors to manufacture professors, who when their turn comes, will manufacture professors.

SIMONE WEIL

We live in an age when pizza gets to your house before the police do.

JEFF MARDER

Whatever starts in California unfortunately has an inclination to spread.

JIMMY CARTER

Is fuel efficiency really what we need most desperately? I say what we really need is a car that can be shot when it breaks down.

RUSSELL BAKER

Living in New York is like coming all the time.

GENE SIMMONS

The most likely way for the world to
be destroyed, most experts agree, is by accident.
That's where we come in; we're computer
professionals. We cause accidents.

NATHANIEL BORENSTEIN

Tip the world over on its side and everything loose
will land in Los Angeles.

FRANK LLOYD WRIGHT

If the automobile had followed the same
development as the computer, a Rolls-Royce
would today cost $100, get a million miles
per gallon, and explode once a year,
killing everyone inside.

NICK JOB

There are more fools in the world
than there are people.

HEINRICH HEINE

There are two million interesting people in New
York and only seventy-eight in Los Angeles.

NEIL SIMON

Man is a puny, slow, awkward, unarmed animal.

JACOB BRONOWSKI

There is nothing more contemptible than a bald
man who pretends to have hair.

MARTIAL, FIRST CENTURY A.D.

Venice would be a fine city if it were only drained.

ULYSSES S. GRANT (ATTRIBUTED)

Incessant company is as bad as
solitary confinement.

VIRGINIA WOOLF

I have often relied on the blindness of strangers.

ADRIENNE E. GUSOFF

Everyone is as God made him,
and often a great deal worse.

MIGUEL DE CERVANTES

I loathe people who keep dogs. They are cowards
who haven't got the guts to bite people themselves.

AUGUST STRINDBERG

If people turn to look at you on the street,
you are not well dressed.

BEAU BRUMMELL

Good taste and humor are a
contradiction in terms, like a chaste whore.

MALCOLM MUGGERIDGE

Applause is but a fart, the crude blast
of the fickle multitude.

WIT AND DROLLERY, 1645

The people are to be taken in small doses.

RALPH WALDO EMERSON

I wish people who have trouble communicating
would just shut up.

TOM LEHRER

The sad truth is that excellence
makes people nervous.

SHANA ALEXANDER, AMERICAN NEWS COMMENTATOR

When science finally locates the center
of the universe, some people will be surprised
to learn they're not it.

ANONYMOUS

Ninety-nine percent of the people in the world
are fools and the rest of us are in
great danger of contagion.

THORNTON WILDER

Spain imports tourists and
exports chambermaids.

CARLOS FUENTES

• CHAPTER 9 •

THE OPIUM OF THE PEOPLE

GOD AND RELIGION, PHILOSOPHY
AND KNOWLEDGE

I know so many things I'm afraid to find out.

JOSEPH HELLER

I don't believe in God because
I don't believe in Mother Goose.

CLARENCE DARROW

There are some ideas so wrong that only a
very intelligent person could believe them.

GEORGE ORWELL

Philosophy: a route of many roads
leading from nowhere to nothing.

AMBROSE BIERCE

I still say a church steeple with a lightning rod
on top shows a lack of confidence.

DOUG MACLEOD

The Bible contains six admonishments
to homosexuals and 362 admonishments
to heterosexuals. That doesn't mean that
God doesn't love heterosexuals. It's just that
they need more supervision.

LYNN LAVNER

God is a comedian playing to an audience
too afraid to laugh.

VOLTAIRE

It has yet to be proven that intelligence
has any survival value.

ARTHUR C. CLARKE

There are only two truly infinite things,
the universe and stupidity. And I am unsure
about the universe.

ALBERT EINSTEIN

If you talk to God, you are praying;
if God talks to you, you have schizophrenia.

THOMAS SZASZ

Ignorance of one's misfortunes is clear gain.

EURIPIDES

My theology, briefly, is that the universe
was dictated but not signed.

CHRISTOPHER MORLEY

I can't understand why people are frightened
of new ideas. I'm frightened of the old ones.

JOHN CAGE

God made everything out of nothing,
but the nothingness shows through.

PAUL VALÉRY

It takes a lot of time to be a genius, you have to sit around so much doing nothing, really doing nothing.

GERTRUDE STEIN

The lord is not my shepherd. I shall want.

MAY SARTON

There is no statement so absurd
that no philosopher will make it.

CICERO

Faith is believing what you know ain't so.

MARK TWAIN

What if nothing exists and we're all in
somebody's dream? Or what's worse, what if
only that fat guy in the third row exists?

WOODY ALLEN

No man with any sense of humor
ever founded a religion.

ROBERT G. INGERSOLL

Thanks to God, I am still an atheist.

LUIS BUÑUEL

There is no record in history of a happy philosopher.

H. L. MENCKEN

The Bible says that the last thing God made
was woman. He must have made her on
Saturday night—it shows fatigue.

ALEXANDRE DUMAS

Religion is what keeps the poor
from murdering the rich.

NAPOLEON BONAPARTE

Man invented language to satisfy
his deep need to complain.

LILY TOMLIN

A Jewish man with parents alive is a
fifteen-year-old boy, and will remain a
fifteen-year-old boy until *they die!*

PHILIP ROTH

A dead atheist is someone who's all dressed up
with no place to go.

JAMES DUFFEY

The little I know I owe to my ignorance.

SACHA GUITRY

The world is proof that God is a committee.

BOB STOKES

Man has made use of his intelligence;
he invented stupidity.

REMY DE GOURMANT

Russia has abolished God, but so far
God has been more tolerant.

JOHN CAMERON SWAYZE, TELEVISION ANCHORMAN

You can always borrow a corkscrew from a member
of the Protestant Episcopal Church.

CHAUNCEY DEPEW

Man's mind, once stretched by a new idea,
never regains its original dimensions.

OLIVER WENDELL HOLMES, JR.

God is always on the side of the heaviest battalions.

VOLTAIRE

The trouble with born-again Christians is that they are an even bigger pain the second time around.

HERB CAEN, AMERICAN JOURNALIST AND AUTHOR

Everything is a dangerous drug except reality, which is unendurable.

CYRIL CONNOLLY

Never believe anything until it has been officially denied.

CLAUD COCKBURN

It is necessary for men to be deceived in religion.

MARCUS TERENTIUS VARRO, ROMAN WRITER

Even if you do learn to speak correct English, whom are you going to speak it to?

CLARENCE DARROW

Our only hope rests on the off-chance
that God does exist.

ALICE THOMAS ELLIS

Every absurdity has a champion to defend it.

OLIVER GOLDSMITH

Like most intellectuals, he is immensely stupid.

MARQUISE DE MERTEUIL

If God lived on earth, people would
break his windows.

JEWISH PROVERB

When a true genius appears in the world you
may know him by this sign: that all the dunces
are in confederacy against him.

JONATHAN SWIFT

Satan probably wouldn't have talked so big
if God had been his wife.

P. J. O'ROURKE

It is dangerous to be sincere
unless you are also stupid.

GEORGE BERNARD SHAW

I not only use all the brains that I have,
but all that I can borrow.

WOODROW WILSON

God is not dead but alive and working on
a less ambitious project.

ANONYMOUS

God is silent, now if we can only get Man to shut up.

WOODY ALLEN

Those who flee temptation generally
leave a forwarding address.

LANE OLINGHOUSE

If other people are going to talk,
conversation becomes impossible.

JAMES MCNEILL WHISTLER

Theology is the effort to explain the unknowable
in terms of the not worth knowing.

H. L. MENCKEN

Why is it that wherever I go,
the resident idiot heads straight for me?

GWYNN THOMAS

I hate quotations. Tell me what you know.

RALPH WALDO EMERSON

No one really listens to anyone else,
and if you try it for a while you'll see why.

MIGNON MCLAUGHLIN

Is man one of God's blunders or is God
one of man's blunders?

NIETZSCHE

A child of five would understand this.
Send someone to fetch a child of five.

GROUCHO MARX

Genius may have its limitations,
but stupidity is not thus handicapped.

ELBERT HUBBARD

The religion of one age is the
literary entertainment of the next.

RALPH WALDO EMERSON

• CHAPTER 10 •

FOOD AND DRINK, HEALTH AND LEISURE

Golf is a good walk spoiled.

MARK TWAIN

I can't cook. I use a smoke alarm as a timer.

CAROL SUSKIND

I've often wondered what goes into a hot dog.
Now I know and I wish I didn't.

WILLIAM ZINSSER

I drink to make other people more interesting.

GEORGE JEAN NATHAN, CRITIC

A doctor's reputation is made by the number
of eminent men who die under his care.

GEORGE BERNARD SHAW

The dying process begins the minute we are born,
but it accelerates during dinner parties.

CAROL MATHAU

I was once thrown out of a mental hospital
for depressing the other patients.

OSCAR LEVANT

The hard part about being a bartender is
figuring out who is drunk and who is just stupid.

RICHARD BRAUNSTEIN

If this is coffee, please bring me some tea.
If this is tea, please bring me some coffee.

ABRAHAM LINCOLN

Beauty is in the eye of the beerholder.

W. C. FIELDS

If I put on five more pounds
I will be eligible for statehood.

AUDREY BUSLIK

I don't jog. If I die I want to be sick.

ABE LEMONS

You don't eat Mexican food—you just rent it.

ALEXEI SAYLE

I hate the outdoors. To me the outdoors
is where the car is.

WILL DURST

It's pretty sad when a person has to
lose weight to play Babe Ruth.

JOHN GOODMAN

I know a man who gave up smoking, drinking, sex, and rich food. He was healthy right up to the time he killed himself.

JOHNNY CARSON

I hate all sports as rabidly as a person who likes sports hates common sense.

H. L. MENCKEN

Most vegetarians I ever see looked enough like their food to be classed as cannibals.

FINLEY PETER DUNNE

Americans can eat garbage, provided you sprinkle it liberally with ketchup, mustard, chili sauce, Tabasco sauce, cayenne pepper, or any other condiment which destroys the original flavor of the dish.

HENRY MILLER

God was an alcoholic. He created the world
when he woke up with a hangover.

PETER COOK

A gourmet is just a glutton with brains.

PHILIP W. HARBERMAN, JR.

Even though a number of people have tried,
no one has yet found a way to drink for a living.

JEAN KERR

And you thought you didn't like people on land...

CAROL LEIFER, ON CRUISE SHIPS

I envy people who drink—at least they know
what to blame everything on.

OSCAR LEVANT

A cucumber should be well sliced and dressed with pepper and vinegar, and then thrown out, as good for nothing.

SAMUEL JOHNSON

There are two classes of travel— first class, and with children.

ROBERT BENCHLEY

A man described as a "sportsman" is generally a bookmaker who takes actresses to nightclubs.

JIMMY CANNON, SPORTSWRITER

With this so-called nouvelle cuisine there is nothing on your plate and plenty on your bill.

PAUL BOCUSE

R & R

I went on a diet, swore off drinking and heavy
eating, and in fourteen days I lost two weeks.

JOE E. LEWIS

Ask your child what he wants for dinner
only if he's buying.

FRAN LEBOWITZ, AMERICAN WRITER AND HUMORIST

Do you know what doctors call teenage
motorcyclists? Organ donors.

PATRICK MURRAY

The trouble with referees is that
they just don't care which side wins.

TOM CANTERBURY

I die by the help of too many physicians.

ALEXANDER THE GREAT

My mother's menu consisted of two choices:
Take it or leave it.

BUDDY HACKETT

I have a great diet. You're allowed to eat anything
you want, but you must eat it with naked fat people.

ED BLUESTONE

It is a good idea to "shop around" before you
settle on a doctor. Ask about the condition of
his Mercedes. Ask about the competence
of his mechanic. Don't be shy! After all,
you're paying for it.

DAVE BARRY

I'm at the age where food has taken
the place of sex in my life. In fact, I've just had
a mirror put over my kitchen table.

RODNEY DANGERFIELD

Never go to a doctor whose office plants have died.

ERMA BOMBECK

I believe every human has a finite number
of heartbeats. I don't intend to waste any of mine.

NEIL ARMSTRONG, AMERICAN ASTRONAUT

When I read about the evils of drinking,
I gave up reading.

HENNY YOUNGMAN

Football incorporates the two worst elements
of American society: violence punctuated
by committee meetings.

GEORGE F. WILL, JOURNALIST AND POLITICAL COMMENTATOR

God heals and the doctor takes the fee.

BENJAMIN FRANKLIN

The second day of a diet is always easier than the first. By the second day you're off it.

JACKIE GLEASON

The most remarkable thing about my mother is that for thirty years she served nothing but leftovers. The original meal has never been found.

CALVIN TRILLIN

I get my exercise acting as a pallbearer to my friends who exercise.

CHAUNCEY DEPEW

The average, healthy, well-adjusted adult gets up at seven-thirty in the morning feeling just plain terrible.

JEAN KERR

Time is an illusion. Lunchtime doubly so.

DOUGLAS ADAMS, AMERICAN WRITER

Finish your vegetables! There are thousands
of children in Hollywood with eating disorders.

JOHN CALLAGHAN

At my age travel broadens the behind.

STEPHEN FRY

In restaurants, the hardness of the butter
increases in direct proportion to the softness
of the bread being served.

HARRIET MARKMAN

I'm not into working out. My philosophy:
No pain, no pain.

CAROL LEIFER

I don't even butter my bread;
I consider that cooking.

KATHERINE CEBRIAN

There's a fine line between fishing
and standing on the shore like an idiot.

STEVEN WRIGHT

Beauty is only skin deep,
and the world is full of thin-skinned people.

RICHARD ARMOUR

God sends meat—the Devil sends cooks.

CHARLES VI

I used to think the only use for sports was to give
small boys something else to kick besides me.

KATHERINE WHITEHORN

When one realizes that his life is worthless
he either commits suicide or travels.

EDWARD DAHLBERG

Airplane travel is nature's way of making you
look like your passport photo.

AL GORE

Coffee in England is just toasted milk.

CHRISTOPHER FRY, PLAYWRIGHT

Most turkeys taste better the day after;
my mother's tasted better the day before.

RITA RUDNER

A perpetual holiday is a good
working definition of hell.

GEORGE BERNARD SHAW

The best way to lose weight is to get
the flu and take a trip to Egypt.

ROZ LAWRENCE

Conversation is the enemy
of good wine and food.

ALFRED HITCHCOCK

CHAPTER 11

LAST WORDS AND EPITAPHS

Good-bye, everybody!

HART CRANE, POET, WHO COMMITTED SUICIDE BY
JUMPING OVERBOARD DURING A STEAMSHIP VOYAGE

They couldn't hit an elephant at this dist—

GENERAL JOHN B. SEDGWICK

OWEN MOORE:
Gone Away
Owin' More
Than He Could Pay

EPITAPH, LONDON, ENGLAND

We who are about to die, are going to take one hell
of a lot of the bastards with us.

JOEL ROSENBERG

God bless . . . God damn.

JAMES THURBER

At last I am going to be well!

PAUL SACRON, FRENCH POET

I owe much: I have nothing;
the rest I leave to the poor.

FRANÇOIS RABELAIS

I feel nothing, apart from a certain difficulty in
continuing to exist.

BERNARD DE FONTENELLE

RETURNED—UNOPENED

EPITAPH OF NORTH CAROLINA SPINSTER POSTMISTRESS

I do not have to forgive my enemies,
I have had them all shot.

RAMON MARIA NAVAREZ, SPANISH GENERAL

Thank heavens the sun has gone in and
I don't have to go out and enjoy it.

LOGAN PEARSAL SMITH, AMERICAN WRITER

I expect I shall have to die beyond my means.

**OSCAR WILDE, ACCEPTING A GLASS OF CHAMPAGNE
ON HIS DEATHBED**

I have had no real gratification or enjoyment
of any sort more than my neighbor on the
next block who is worth only half a million.

WILLIAM HENRY VANDERBILT

Everybody has got to die, but I have always
believed an exception would be made
in my case. Now what?

WILLIAM SAROYAN

I'm so bored with it all.

WINSTON CHURCHILL

Life is too short to learn German.

RICHARD PORSON, BRITISH CLASSICIST

My work is done. Why wait?

GEORGE EASTMAN, KODAK FOUNDER, IN A SUICIDE NOTE

If this is dying, then I don't think much of it.

LYTTON STRACHEY

I have had just about all I can take of myself.

S. N. BEHRMAN, ON REACHING THE AGE OF SEVENTY-FIVE

Psychics will lead dogs to your body.

FORTUNE COOKIE

Harry Edsel Smith
1903–1942
Looked up the elevator shaft to see
if the car was coming down.
It was.

EPITAPH, ALBANY, NEW YORK

Life is a jest and all things show it.
I thought so once and now I know it.

EPITAPH, JOHN GAY, ENGLISH POET

BIBLIOGRAPHY

Andrews, Robert, ed. *The Concise Columbia Dictionary of Quotations*. New York: Columbia University Press, 1989.

———. *Famous Lines: a Columbia Dictionary of Familiar Quotations.* New York: Columbia University Press, 1997.

Augarde, Tony, ed. *The Oxford Dictionary of Modern Quotations*. New York: Oxford University Press, 1991.

Barkin, George, ed. *The Sardonic Humor of Ambrose Bierce*. New York: Dover, 1963.

Baron, Joseph L., ed. *A Treasury of Jewish Quotations*. Northvale, NJ: Jason Aronson, 1985.

Barry, Dave. *Dave Barry's Complete Guide to Guys*. New York: Random House, 1995.

Bell, Janet Cheatham, ed. *Famous Black Quotations*. New York: Warner Books, 1994.

Bierce, Ambrose. *The Devil's Dictionary*. New York: Dover, 1958.

Bohle, Bruce, ed. *The Home Book of American Quotations*. New York: Dodd, Mead & Company, 1967.

Bolander, Donald O., ed. *Instant Quotation Dictionary*. Danbury, CT: Franklin-Watts, 1986.

Brallier, Jess, and Sally Chabert. *Presidential Wit and Wisdom: Maxims, Mottoes, Sound Bites, Speeches, and Asides—Memorable Quotes from America's Presidents.* New York: Penguin, 1996.

Brussell, Eugene E., ed. *Webster's New World Dictionary of Quotable Definitions* (2d ed.). New York: Simon & Schuster, 1970.

Burke, John Gordon, and Ned Kehde, eds. *Dictionary of Contemporary Quotations* (3d revised ed.). John Gordon Burke Publishers, Inc., 1994.

Byrne, Robert. *1,911 Best Things Anybody Ever Said*. New York: Fawcett, 1988.

Charlton, James, ed. *The Executive's Quotation Book*. New York: St. Martin's Press, 1993.

Cohen, J. M., and M. J. Cohen, eds. *The Penguin Dictionary of Modern Quotations* (2d ed.). New York: Penguin, 1980.

Cole, William, and Louis Phillips, eds. *Sex: Even More Fun You Can Have Without Laughing*. Edison, NJ: Castle Books, 1997.

——. *Sex: The Most Fun You Can Have Without Laughing*. Edison, NJ: Castle Books, 1997.

Contradictory Quotations. Burnt Mill, England: Longman, 1983.

Crainer, Stuart, ed. *The Ultimate Book of Business Quotations*. New York: AMACOM, 1998.

Crawley, Tony, ed. *Chambers Film Quotes*. New York: Chambers, 1991.

Curruth, Gorton, and Eugene Ehrlich, eds. *The Giant Book of American Quotations*. New York: Portland House, 1988.

Donadio, Stephen, et al., eds. *The New York Public Library Book of Twentieth Century Quotations*. New York: Warner, 1992.

Esar, Evan, ed. *20,000 Quips and Quotes*. New York: Doubleday, 1968.

Fadiman, Clifton, ed. *The Little, Brown Book of Anecdotes*. Boston: Little, Brown, 1985.

Fergusson, Rosalind, ed. *The Penguin Dictionary of Proverbs*. New York: Penguin, 1983.

Fitzhenry, Robert I., ed. *The Barnes & Noble Book of Quotations*. New York: Barnes & Noble, 1981.

Fleisch, Rudolf, ed. *The New Book of Unusual Quotations*. New York: Harper & Row, 1966.

Frank, Leonard Roy, ed. *Random House Webster's Quotationary*. New York: Random House, 1999.

Goodman, Dan, ed. *Meditations for a Miserable Millennium: Daily Affirmations for Staying Hopeless and Unhappy in the Year 2000 and Beyond*. New York: St. Martin's, 1996.

Green, Jonathon, ed. *The Cassell Dictionary of Cynical Quotations*. London: Cassell, 1994.

Henry, Lewis C., ed. *Best Quotations for All Occasions*. New York: Ballentine, 1955.

Isaacs, Alan, ed. *Cassell Dictionary of Sex Quotations*. London: Market House Books, 1993.

Jarman, Colin, ed. *The Guiness Book of Poisonous Quotes*. Chicago: Contemporary Books, 1991.

Knowles, Elizabeth, ed. *The Oxford Dictionary of Quotations* (5th ed.). New York: Oxford University Press, 1999.

Lansky, Bruce, ed. *Lovesick: The Best Quotations about Love and Sex*. New York: Meadowbrook Press, 1996.

Lebowitz, Fran. *Metropolitan Life*. New York: Dutton, 1978.

————. *Social Studies*. New York: Random House, 1981.

Lieberman, Gerald F., ed. *3,500 Good Quotes for Speakers*. New York: Doubleday, 1983.

Machale, Des, ed. *Wit: Humorous Quotations from Woody Allen to Oscar Wilde*. New York: Fine Communications, 1999.

The Macmillan Dictionary of Quotations. New York: Macmillan, 1989.

Maggio, Rosalie, comp. *The Beacon Book of Quotations by Women*. Boston: Beacon Press, 1992.

Markoe, Merrill. *Merrill Markoe's Guide to Love*. New York: Grove/Atlantic, 1998.

Marsden, C.R.S, comp. *The Dictionary of Outrageous Quotations*. Topsfield, MA: Salem House, 1988.

McKenzie, Carole, ed. *Quotable Sex*. New York: St. Martin's, 1992.

McWilliams, Peter, ed. *The Life 101 Quote Book*. Los Angeles: Prelude Press, 1997.

Mico, Ted, ed. *Life Stinks: A Wry Look of Hopelessness, Despair, and Disaster*. Kansas City: Ariel Books, 1995.

Mieder, Wolfgang, ed. *The Prentice-Hall Encyclopedia of World proverbs*. Englewood Cliffs, NJ: Prentice-Hall, 1986.

Murphy, Edward F., ed. *2,715 One-Line Quotations for Speakers, Writers and Raconteurs*. New York: Random House, 1989.

Newman, Amanda, ed. *Women Are from Venus, Men Are from Hell*. Holbrook, MA: Adams Media Corporation, 1999.

Nowlan, Robert A., and Gwendolyn W. Nowlan, eds. *Film Quotations*. Jefferson, NC: McFarland & Co., 1994.

O'Connor, Joey. *Women Are Always Right and Men Are Never Wrong*. Nashville, TN: Word Publishing, 1999.

101 Reasons Not to Do Anything: A Collection of Cynical and Defeatist Quotations. West Sussex, England: Summersdale, 1998.

Paglia, Camille. *Sex, Art, and American Culture*. New York: Vintage, 1992.

Parker, Dorothy. *The Portable Dorothy Parker*. New York: Viking, 1973.

Partnow, Elaine, ed. *The Quotable Woman*. New York: Facts On File, 1992.

Peter, Laurence J., ed. *Peter's Quotations: Ideas for Our Time*. New York: William Morrow, 1977.

Petras, Kathryn, and Ross Petras, eds. *The Whole World Book of Quotations*. Reading, MA: Addison-Wesley, 1995.

Phillips, Louis, and William Cole, eds. *The Random House Treasury of Humorous Quotations*. New York: Random House, 1996.

Platt, Suzy, ed. *Respectfully Quoted: A Dictionary of Quotations from the Congressional Research Service*. Washington, DC: Library of Congress, U.S. Government Printing Office, 1989.

Porter, Dahlia, ed. *365 Reflections on Dating*. Holbrook, MA: Adams Media Corporation, 2000.

Quinn, Tracy, ed. *Quotable Women of the Twentieth Century*. New York: William Morrow, 1999.

The Quotable Woman. Philadelphia: Running Press, 1991.

Rando, Catarina, ed. *Words of Women: Quotations for Success*. San Francisco: Power Dynamics Publishing, 1995.

Rasmussen, R. Kent, ed. *The Quotable Mark Twain*. Chicago: Contemporary Books, 1997.

Ratcliffe, Susan, ed. *Oxford Love Quotations*. New York: Oxford University Press, 1999.